ON TRIAL

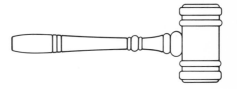

FAMOUS
POLITICAL
TRIALS

ANDREW DAVID

INTRODUCTION BY DAN COHEN

Lerner Publications Company ■ Minneapolis

ACKNOWLEDGMENTS: The illustrations are reproduced through the courtesy of: pp. 4, 42, Documantation Photographique; p. 11, Lauros-Giraudon; pp. 7, 67, 70, U.S. Army Photographs; p. 13, Photographie Bulloz; pp. 16-17, The Corcoran Gallery of Art; p. 20, Photographie Giraudon; p. 22, The Frick Collection; p. 25, Kupferstichkabinett des Kunstmuseums, Basel; p. 26 (left), Photo Alinari; p. 26 (right), National Portrait Gallery; p. 29, British Museum; pp. 34, 40, The New York Public Library; p. 37, Fogg Art Museum, Harvard University, John Witt Randall Collection; p. 46, Culver Pictures, Inc.; pp. 50, 53, Radio Times Hulton Picture Library; pp. 56, 84, YIVO Institute for Jewish Research; pp. 57, 95, The Bettmann Archive, Inc.; pp. 58, 59, National Archives, U.S. Signal Corps Photos; p. 64, National Archives; pp. 74, 77, 80, Religious News Service Photos; p. 90, National Archives, Keystone Photo; pp. 94, 96, 97, 99, Government Press Office, Tel-Aviv; p. 102, Herb Kohn; p. 104, Harper and Row Publishers, Inc.; p. 109, H. J. Lerner; p. 110, Wide World Photos.

Cover art by Bob Klein

Introduction and Chapter 8, *Anatoly Shcharansky*, by Dan Cohen

LIBRARY OF CONGRESS CATALOGING IN PUBLICATION DATA

David, Andrew.
Famous political trials.

(On trial)
Includes index.
SUMMARY: Discusses eight historically important, politically related court cases in which an individual faced an authority, such as a government or church, which misused the courts in attempting to establish its power over the individual.

1. Trials (Political crimes and offenses)—Juvenile literature. [1. Trials (Political crimes and offenses) 2. Civil rights] I. Title. II. Series.

K543.P6W5   1979   345'.02'3   79-16923
ISBN 0-8225-1429-X

Manufactured in the United States of America. Published simultaneously in Canada by J. M. Dent & Sons (Canada) Ltd., Don Mills, Ontario.

International Standard Book Number: 0-8225-1429-X
Library of Congress Catalog Card Number:79-16923

1 2 3 4 5 6 7 8 9 10 85 84 83 82 81 80

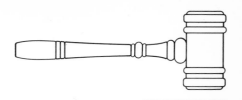

Contents

Introduction 5

1 *Joan of Arc* 8

2 *Sir Thomas More* 23

3 *Galileo Galilei* 33

4 *Captain Alfred Dreyfus* 45

5 *The Nuremberg Trials* 55

6 *Cardinal Joseph Mindszenty* 72

7 *Adolf Eichmann* 82

8 *Anatoly Shcharansky* 101

Index 111

The Italian scientist Galileo appears before officials of the Roman Catholic Church in 1633.

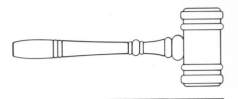

Introduction

There have been many times in world history when the courts have been used to make a political point rather than simply to settle disputes or to try persons accused of breaking the law. Each of the court cases you are going to read about in this book involves the use of the courts by an authority, such as a government or a church, to establish its power over an individual. In all cases, the individual is someone whose point of view is different from that accepted by the authority. In the 17th-century case of Galileo, for example, the powerful Roman Catholic church brought Galileo to trial because he had voiced ideas about the solar system that were different from those held by the church at that time.

Usually a government or church wants to suppress such an individual in order to protect its own political power or to demonstrate such power to the public. The authority may consider an outspoken individual with an unusual viewpoint a threat to its power and/or security. Thus the authority finds a way to bring the person to trial, in order to stop that person from speaking out or acting in any unacceptable manner. The result is often a "show trial," which the whole world can watch. This gives the authority an opportunity to show that it has the power and control to root out and punish unacceptable behavior. The authority thus makes an example of the person or persons whom it is putting on trial, and effectively warns other people not to make the same mistake.

An authority, however, also takes certain risks when it tries to use the courts for its own political purposes. For one thing, holding the trial in the first place publicizes the very ideas that the authority is trying to suppress. It gives the accused individual a world platform from which to express the ideas for which he or she is being punished.

Also, by throwing all the weight of its power against a single person or handful of people, the authority runs the risk of stirring up the public's sympathy for the accused. The accused person becomes a martyr — a lone individual pitted unfairly against a large, powerful institution.

The authority also risks being criticized by the public for the manner in which the trial is conducted. Sometimes, in its eagerness to bring defendants to trial in a court of law, the authority files absurd or unrealistic charges, which serve merely as a way of getting the person into court. Or the authority may ignore the usual legal requirements, such as proper jurisdiction. Then the authority lays itself open to charges of injustice and improper use of the courts.

In each of the cases you will read about, some or all of these elements of an authority's misuse of the courts are present. Yes, even the Nazi war crimes trials had their critics, for the right of the Allied governments to try

German citizens for acts that were not criminal under German law was questioned by legal scholars.

As demonstrations of the proper working of the law, these cases leave much to be desired. But as political events, they are of great historic importance and should be read with that thought in mind.

DAN COHEN

Nazi war criminals on trial in Nuremberg, Germany, 1945

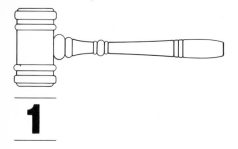

1

Joan of Arc

People called her the "Maid of Orléans." At the age of only 17, Joan of Arc led the army of France against the powerful English armies and defeated them. She helped the rightful king of France to regain his throne. This brave young girl was destined to become a heroine in her own time and a legend in history.

Joan of Arc was born in 1412, in the small village of Domrémy, in the northeastern corner of France. At the time of Joan's birth, France was in the midst of the Hundred Years' War, which was actually a long series of wars, between France and England. At that point in the wars, England was allied with the forces of the French duke of Burgundy, who had turned against France. With his help, the English army had invaded and occupied much of northern France. Charles VII, the *dauphin*, or rightful heir to the throne of France, could not officially be crowned king because the English enemies held the city of Reims, the traditional coronation site. The armies of Charles VII had been unable to drive out the hated English invaders.

It was in this war-torn atmosphere that Joan of Arc, an intelligent and intensely religious person, grew up. She was from a peasant family, and with her parents, her three brothers, and a sister, she worked in the farm fields. But Joan was not an ordinary farm girl.

When Joan was about 13 years old, something very disturbing began to happen to her. She began to have visions, which she believed were from heaven. In the visions, three saints appeared to her — St. Michael, St. Catherine, and St. Margaret — and they talked to her. She became convinced that it was her mission to help save France from the English. The saints directed her to go to Charles VII, the dauphin, and to offer to lead France against its enemies.

In 1429, when Joan was 17, she told her parents what the saints had directed her to do. Then she set out for the castle of Chinon, where the dauphin and his court were residing. Joan dressed herself in men's clothing and cut her hair short, like that of a young man. (She thought that looking like a boy would help her in her mission to reach Charles VII and in leading the soldiers of France. Later, however, it would prove to be one reason for her downfall.) In her "disguise," she made her way through enemy territory to the castle where Charles VII held court.

The dauphin was informed that an "interesting" young girl, who was supposed to be able to speak with the saints, wished to see him. Not knowing whether she was crazy or a saint herself, he decided to admit her. The dauphin, however, disguised himself as just another member of the court. If this was intended as a test, Joan passed it easily. When she entered the royal chambers, she went directly to Charles VII, ignoring the rest of the group in the court, and knelt before him to explain her mission.

Joan was then questioned for several weeks by the dauphin's advisors on religious and state matters. Apparently they were impressed with her, because they advised the dauphin to do what she suggested.

Joan of Arc, still only 17 years old, was outfitted in her own suit of armor and given command of a small division of the dauphin's troops. She set out almost immediately to march on Orléans, a very important French city that had fallen to the English. As she rode through the countryside, word about this remarkable young girl spread quickly. Many of the soldiers believed that she had been sent directly by God to lead them to victory, and they willingly followed her into battle at Orléans. The troops were also inspired by her bravery and impressed by her brilliant battle strategy. The English fell in defeat, and they fled the city. The great success of this young girl was soon known throughout all of France. People called her the "Maid of Orléans" and spoke of her with the respect reserved for conquering heroes.

After Orléans, Joan led the French to victory in four more battles. She was wounded twice, but she recovered and went on fighting. Finally, Joan returned in triumph to the dauphin and urged him to let her lead him into Reims. Together, she said, they would conquer the city so that Charles could be consecrated and crowned the true king of France.

The dauphin agreed. As they made their way toward Reims, the French troops, led by Joan, battled through town after town. Everywhere the people in the towns and villages rose up to join Joan in battle, and one by one, they regained the towns. The English and the Burgundians

Joan of Arc, the Maid of Orléans

retreated. At Reims, the enemy had already fled by the time Joan and Charles arrived.

On July 17, 1429, with Joan by his side, Charles VII was formally crowned king of France in the cathedral at Reims. But the Hundred Years' War was far from over. Paris itself was still in the hands of the enemy, as were many other French cities. At the orders of King Charles, Joan of Arc continued to fight for France. Although her attack on Paris was unsuccessful, she kept on fighting.

In May 1430, word reached Joan that the city of Compiègne had fallen to the forces of the duke of Burgundy. She went there immediately and, in the dark of night, made her way unnoticed into the besieged town. The next day she rallied the townspeople to fight against the Burgundians. Joan and her makeshift army fought bravely, but finally they were forced to retreat. As they did, Joan was knocked from her horse and captured by John of Luxembourg, a high-ranking officer of the duke of Burgundy.

Joan was taken to John of Luxembourg's castle and imprisoned there. She tried to escape, but she was unsuccessful. She was then moved to another castle and locked into one of its towers. Again she tried to escape, this time by leaping from a high window into the moat below. But she was recaptured before she could get away.

The capture of Joan of Arc was a feather in the cap of the enemy forces. In one short year, they had become quite concerned with the impact that this young woman was having on the course of the war. At last they had stopped her.

But the English wanted her in their own custody, rather than in that of the Burgundians. They also wanted her dead, to insure that she could never again lead the French

This 15th-century illustration by an unknown artist shows Joan as a prisoner of the Burgundians.

forces against them. The English approached Joan's captor. At first, the duke of Burgundy was not so willing to give up his prize prisoner. But when the English offered him a very substantial sum of money, he agreed to part with her.

The English king, Henry VI, knew that he could not simply execute Joan of Arc. For one thing, it was against the rules of war. If the English killed a prisoner of war like Joan, the French could do the same to an important English prisoner. Another, and perhaps more important, reason for not killing Joan was the fact that she was a heroine throughout France. Executing her in cold blood would undoubtedly rouse the French people to fight even harder because it would make her a martyr in their eyes.

13

That the English did not want. But they did want her dead and out of the way.

King Henry VI of England decided that, first, Joan would have to be disgraced and discredited at a public trial. Then he could "legitimately" have her executed.

The problem was, however, that Joan of Arc had not committed any crimes against the government. So it was decided that she should be tried for crimes against the church.

In Joan's time — the latter part of the Middle Ages — the Catholic church was extremely powerful. The greatest crime that a person could commit was *heresy* — the crime of holding beliefs that were different from the established doctrines of the church. To search out heretics, or non-believers, the church appointed officials called *inquisitors*. It was the mission of these men not only to find the heretics but also to try them for their crimes and to mete out their punishments.

Torture was an accepted method used by the inquisitors to interrogate suspects. The "trial" given to an accused heretic was usually nothing more than a public reading of the charges and of the confession that had been obtained through torture. This was quickly followed by the reading of the sentence, usually death. All over Europe, people feared the terrible powers of the church and the inquisitors.

The English decided to enlist the aid of the inquisitors in their case against Joan. The plan was for the church to try to convict her as a heretic, and then to turn her over to the state authorities — the English — for punishment.

Two judges were put in charge of Joan's case. The first was a corrupt bishop named Pierre Cauchon, who had sided with the English before. As a second judge, the

English appointed a much-feared inquisitor named Jean Le Maistre. He also favored the English, under whom he exercised his authority in Paris. Together, the two judges drew up a list of 70 charges against Joan of Arc. Today some of these charges sound wildly absurd. But at the time they were made, they were serious issues. The main points in the case were —

> that Joan of Arc had sinned against the church by dealing with God directly instead of through the clergy;

> that Joan of Arc had claimed to be directed by God through visions of three saints but could not prove it, and that therefore she had blasphemed, or mocked the church, by telling a lie.

The judges planned to interrogate Joan carefully on these main points, as well as on many others. Their aim, of course, was to get her to publicly confess her guilt. But as Bishop Cauchon and Jean Le Maistre were to find out, this would not be an easy task.

Joan of Arc was held in prison, chained most of the time, and kept under constant guard. There she was interrogated, and the questioning was long and rigorous. Although the inquisitors did not use torture at this point, they kept up constant pressure on Joan. She was repeatedly asked to confess her guilt of crimes against God and especially against the church. Time and again she refused. She also refused to give her captors any information about her dealings and conversations with King Charles VII.

When she was not being questioned, Joan was continually threatened and mistreated by her guards. On several occasions they even tried to rape her.

The Trial of Joan of Arc, from a series of paintings done by a 19th-century French artist

Throughout her ordeal, Joan was completely alone. Cowardly King Charles did not even come to her aid. She had only herself — no lawyer or advisor — on which to rely. Yet she would not "confess" anything.

Finally, the judges had no course left but to conduct a trial without the confession. So in March 1431, they drew up formal charges. They were forced to reduce the number of charges from the original 70 to 12. These were the only ones for which they felt there were any grounds whatsoever.

In addition to the two points stated earlier, which were the core of the case, they charged —

that Joan of Arc wore men's clothing and had her hair cut short;

that Joan of Arc attempted to foretell the future
by predicting that France would defeat England;
that Joan of Arc had the boldness to claim that
St. Michael had spoken to her in French instead
of in the "proper" language, English.

The charges were written up and sent to the University
of Paris, where a panel of religious scholars was to rule
on them. The scholars, however, were very clearly under
the domination of the English, and it was obvious from
the outset what their decision would be.

As the difficult weeks before the trial wore on, the bad
treatment Joan received made her weaker and weaker.
Finally she became seriously ill. The inquisitors began to
fear that she might die in prison, and that was precisely

what the English did *not* want. The young girl would surely be viewed as a martyr by the French if she died in prison as a result of mistreatment. The inquisitors hastily gave her medical care and improved her living conditions, and she recovered.

Before bringing Joan to public trial, the inquisitors decided to try one last method of forcing a "confession" — the threat of torture. Joan was taken down to the basement of the castle where she was imprisoned. There she was shown some of the instruments that could be used to make her confess. These were the common torture instruments of the day — the rack that stretched a human body until the arms and legs were torn from their sockets, and the boards and weights that were piled across the stomach and chest to slowly crush a person to death.

Joan stood firm. She said that she had simply done what she had been directed to do by God through the words of his saints. Therefore, she said, she could not confess to any wrongdoing. Even torture at its cruelest could not make her change her mind. And if, because of the pain and her human weakness, she should give in and confess, she said she would later deny her confession. The judges, apparently seeing that she could not be moved, abandoned the idea of torture.

Then word was finally received from Paris that the religious scholars had reached a decision in the case of Joan of Arc. To no one's surprise, she was found guilty on all counts.

Without the all-important confession, the English still felt that executing her would be risky. Nevertheless, it was announced that the results of her trial and her sentencing would be read publicly on May 24, 1431. On that day, Joan was taken to a cemetery under heavy guard to face the judges. Nearby was the execution stake, fully prepared for burning her to death. The charges and the guilty verdict were read to her. She was told then that she should make a public *abjuration*, or confession. In it, she could renounce her past sins and promise never to commit them again. If she made the abjuration, she would be spared death by burning.

Joan asked instead that the charges and verdict be sent to Rome to be ruled on by the pope himself. But her request was refused.

Many persons begged her to make the abjuration to save her life. Under the shadow of the stake and the executioner, she finally agreed to sign her name to the public confession. The court sentenced her to life imprisonment. But the English were unsatisfied. They had not gotten the death penalty they had wanted.

Joan was taken back to prison. A few days later, however, she was found dressed once again in men's clothing. This had been one of the "crimes" that she had promised not to commit again. Some say that she was forced by her guards to put on these clothes. But when Bishop Cauchon and other authorities were brought in to view her, Joan said simply but firmly that the saints had told her she had done wrong by signing the abjuration. She took back her confession.

She was again pronounced a heretic — now an unforgiven one. A new sentence for having "relapsed" into her criminal and sinful ways was delivered. She was to be executed.

On May 30, 1431, Joan of Arc, now 19 years old, was taken to the marketplace in the city of Rouen, France. There, before the eyes of the townspeople, she was tied to the stake. Beneath her were huge bales of kindling

Convicted of being a heretic, Joan of Arc was burned at the stake on May 30, 1431.

wood. To one side stood the executioner, a burning torch in his hand. In the back of the crowd was a priest whom Joan had asked to hold high a crucifix for her to look at in her last moments of life. And with her eyes on that crucifix, Joan of Arc was burned to death at the stake.

The English and Burgundians, however, accomplished nothing for themselves by executing Joan of Arc. As they had feared, she was looked upon as a martyr, and her life and tragic death inspired the French forces. Largely because of Joan of Arc, the tide of the long Hundred Years' War was turned in favor of the French. A short four years after Joan's death, the powerful duke of Burgundy withdrew from the English and came back to fight for France. The king of France, Charles VII, recaptured the city of Paris. Eighteen years after Joan's death, the war finally ended, and France regained all its territory.

After the war, Joan of Arc was exonerated of all her "sins" and "crimes." In 1920 she was formally declared a saint by the Catholic church.

In her short life of 19 years, Joan of Arc helped to change the course of her country's history. Today she remains a vivid example of the courage and dignity of a lone individual pitted against a corrupt and powerful institution.

A portrait of Thomas More by his friend, the artist Hans Holbein the Younger

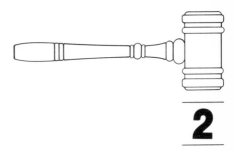

2

Thomas More

In a court of law in London, England, Sir Thomas More stood before the lord chancellor, the highest judge in the land. Sir Thomas had once held that important position himself. Now a convicted traitor to king and country, he stood and listened to the lord chancellor read his sentence — slow death by torture.

Thomas More was taken back to his prison room in the Tower of London. For the moment, however, his terrible sentence was not carried out. The sentence had to be approved by his one-time friend King Henry VIII of England before any action could be taken.

This was a sad state of affairs for Thomas More, who had risen from humble origins to become one of the most well-known and highly respected men in England. He was a man of great brilliance, strength of character, and dedication to principle. Strangely enough, these qualities, which had enabled him to reach his high position in the English realm, were also to be his downfall.

Thomas More was born in 1478 in London. His father, a judge, sent him to Oxford University. After graduation, he studied law. As a young man, More was interested in everything — law, government, religion, philosophy, and the arts. He remained a scholar throughout his life. In later years he was a great patron of the arts and counted among his friends the painter Hans Holbein the Younger and the great humanist Erasmus. More himself was a well-known writer. He produced works in the areas of history and law, and he even wrote English and Latin poetry. One of his greatest books, *Utopia*, is an account of an imaginary ideal society in which everything is just and everyone is equal under the law. *Utopia* is now considered a classic work of English literature.

Thomas More also produced a long series of writings about religion and the church. Like most English citizens of his day, he was a Roman Catholic. To More, religion was a central part of existence. He often felt a need to withdraw from the world into the spiritual life. He preferred to live simply and shunned many worldly pleasures. More acknowledged that a life of religious devotion was not always easy. As he put it, "We may not look...to go to heaven in feather beds. It is not the way." With that idea in mind, he led a life of discipline and self-sacrifice; he even wore a scratchy, uncomfortable hair shirt as a mark of self-denial.

Thomas More, however, was also a brilliant and witty man of the world. His shrewd legal mind and capacity for hard work enabled him to rise steadily within the English government. He began as a justice of the peace and progressed rapidly to become a judge, then a diplomat, and then Speaker of the House of Commons in the English Parliament. In 1529, at the age of 51, he was

Hans Holbein the Younger made this sketch of Thomas More and his family in 1526.

appointed lord chancellor by King Henry VIII.

More was the first person appointed to this high position who was not a clergyman or a nobleman. From his powerful new office, he headed the judicial branch of the government and presided over the House of Lords.

As lord chancellor, More worked closely with King Henry. The two men grew to like each other, for they had much in common. King Henry VIII was a shrewd and powerful politician and military leader. He was also an accomplished scholar, and so he enjoyed talking with Thomas More on a wide variety of subjects. But at a time of problems and strife in England their friendship was destined to break down. King Henry was involved in a serious argument with the Catholic church. He wanted the church to annul his 20-year marriage to Catherine

King Henry VIII   Anne Boleyn

of Aragon. She had not borne him a son and heir, and besides, he wanted to marry his new love, Anne Boleyn. Henry had appealed to the pope in Rome for special permission to divorce Catherine, but it had not been granted.

In the past, Henry had been a devout Catholic. He had spoken out against Martin Luther in 1521 when Luther had broken from the Catholic church. For that act, the pope had named Henry VIII "Defender of the Faith." Now, however, Henry's loyalty to the pope and to the church began to diminish.

When the annulment of his marriage was not granted, Henry decided to break from the Catholic church. Little by little, the king began to take over the powers of the church in England. He restricted the powers of the priests and bishops and made it known to them that *he* was the ruler of both the church and state in England.

Sir Thomas More could not accept such actions, for he believed strongly in the Catholic church and in the supremacy of the pope in Rome. He did not speak out publicly against what the king was doing, but he did not accept it, either. In May 1532, he quietly resigned as lord chancellor. Though he remained officially silent on the matter, his resignation was viewed throughout England as one of protest.

The following year King Henry appointed a new Archbishop of Canterbury, Thomas Cranmer. As the most powerful representative of the church in England, Cranmer announced that the king's marriage to Catherine was null and void, despite the fact that this pronouncement went directly against the pope's ruling. Henry VIII then took Anne Boleyn as his wife and the new queen of England. Sir Thomas More was invited to attend the wedding and the crowning of the queen. He refused. The king was now growing very angry with his former friend. He took More's absence as another protest and as a personal rebuff.

Soon certain charges were brought against Thomas More. He was accused of accepting bribes and of improper conduct as lord chancellor. The charges could not, however, be proven. They were made in order to damage More's reputation rather than to bring him to court.

In 1534 the showdown came. It was in the form of the Act of Supremacy, which Henry ordered Parliament to enact into law. The act stated that the king of England was the rightful head of the church of England. It denied the supremacy of the pope in Rome. In addition, it required that all leading or important persons in the country sign an oath that acknowledged these facts.

Thomas More refused to sign the oath. He was warned then that if he did not sign it, he would be arrested. More said that he was being placed in an impossible position. If he did not sign the oath, he would be putting his life in grave danger, since not signing would be treason against the king, and treason was punishable by death. If he did sign the oath, however, he would place his soul in danger by going against God's church. He chose not to sign.

Furious, King Henry had More arrested and imprisoned in the Tower of London. But he hesitated at the thought of trying and executing his friend. More was too well known and well respected in England simply to be "disposed of." In addition, Henry really wanted More to agree with him. He wanted it partly because it would be a strong endorsement of his own actions before the world, and partly because he respected More's great mind and wanted his friend's approval. The king sent several different people to talk to More, to try to persuade him to change his views and sign the oath. But it was not to be. More still refused.

The king spent a year trying, unsuccessfully, to persuade More. Finally, he decided to make an example of a number of Catholic monks and of Bishop John Fisher, a friend of More's who had also refused to sign the oath. They were quickly brought to trial, convicted, and executed. More was confronted with the king's determination and was offered another chance to give in. Again he refused.

Finally, Henry felt he had no choice. Sir Thomas More was brought to trial in Westminster Hall in London, on July 1, 1535. A special court was appointed to hear the case. Eight judges, presided over by the new lord chancellor, and a jury of 12 noblemen were selected to sit in judgment. The attorney general of England would prosecute the case. More chose to defend himself.

Bishop John Fisher

Four charges were brought against Thomas More. The first and primary one was that he had refused to sign the oath admitting the king's supremacy over the church in England. The second and third charges concerned More's correspondence with Bishop Fisher. Supposedly More had written to encourage the bishop to refuse to sign the oath. The fourth charge was that More had claimed that the English Parliament did not have the authority to make the king the head of the church.

Thomas More was 57 years old when he appeared in court to defend himself. The year in prison had been extremely difficult, and his health was no longer good. His mind, however, was still sharp, and his determination and beliefs were as strong as they had ever been. He still had the finest legal mind in England.

One of the first things Thomas More did in his own defense was to refute the charges regarding his correspondence with the late Bishop Fisher. He demanded that the prosecution exhibit the letters in court. If they did, he said, the letters would clearly show that he, Thomas More, had only suggested that the bishop follow his own conscience. The prosecution declined to produce the evidence, and so those charges were dropped.

The prosecution now said that the most important charge — More's refusal to sign the oath — amounted to a refusal to accept the king as head of the church. Thomas More said that that was not so. In fact, he had neither accepted nor rejected the king's position. He had said nothing either way. Nowhere in the world, he argued, is there any law that makes *silence* punishable. If he had by his words or actions done something against the law, he could be tried for those words or actions. But how could the fact that he had said or done *nothing* be construed as a crime?

The prosecutor did not agree. According to English common law, he claimed, loyalty required a subject to confirm the law freely.

Thomas More quickly pointed out that under English common law it was also written that "silence implies consent." Therefore, according to English law, it should be assumed that his saying nothing showed that he was in agreement. Therefore, the prosecutor could not use the argument from English common law because it would of its very nature prove More innocent of any wrongdoing.

The arguments leaped back and forth. The crucial question still remained. Was Sir Thomas More required to sign the oath? Despite More's brilliant defense, the judges and jury deemed that he was. After only a very short deliberation, they rendered a verdict of guilty.

After the verdict was read, Sir Thomas More asked if he could speak on his own behalf. This privilege was in the tradition of the English court, he said, and he would appreciate the chance to speak his mind before hearing his sentence.

He now broke his "silence." Thomas More spoke strongly and clearly of his beliefs. He said that in all his studies over the years he had never once found anything to justify making a layman, or nonmember of the clergy, head of the church. In addition, he had discovered nothing that enabled the state to usurp the powers of the church and to assume the church's powers and duties. Such actions were against the will of God, the church, and his own personal beliefs. Therefore, he could never bring himself to support such actions. He said that one country or kingdom did not have the power to decide the fate of all Christianity. And then he was finished.

The lord chancellor read his gruesome sentence. More was condemned to be hanged, drawn and quartered, and beheaded, with his head displayed on London Bridge. After the sentencing, he was taken back to prison in the Tower of London.

For several days King Henry VIII considered the fate of the man who had once been among his favorite friends. Finally, Thomas More was informed that the king, in his mercy, had modified the sentence to a simple beheading. When told of the king's decision, More said, with typical wit, "God forbid the king should use any more of such mercy to any of my friends."

Less than a week after his trial, Sir Thomas More was brought to the scaffold on a hill near the Tower. A large crowd had gathered to watch the execution of one of

England's most famous persons. Thomas More was led out. Even at this final moment his wit did not desert him. At the steep scaffold steps he told the guard with him, "Assist me up, and in coming down I will shift for myself." He spoke a few last words, concluding with the wish that he would be remembered as having "died the king's good servant but God's first."

The executioner, holding his ax with its huge curved blade, watched as Thomas More placed his head on the block. As the executioner raised the ax, Thomas More said softly to him, "Wait till I put aside my beard, for that never committed treason."

Then the ax fell, and Sir Thomas More was dead. He had not compromised his beliefs, and he had been as brave and dignified as any man could hope to be in the last moment of his life.

Whether Thomas More was correct in his beliefs is something that must be decided by each person according to his or her own ideas. Whether Thomas More was courageous, strong, and moral in his actions and beliefs, however, no one need ever question.

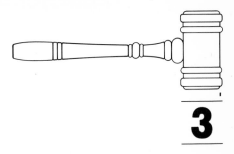

3

Galileo

When great scientific discoveries or new ideas are first put forward, they are not always immediately accepted. People are reluctant to let go of old ideas and beliefs and to take up new ones. Galileo Galilei, a brilliant Italian scientist of the 17th century, learned this truth the hard way. Using objective scientific observation and brilliant deductive reasoning, he made certain discoveries about the sun, the planets, and the earth that showed they were different from what most people then believed them to be. Most people accepted the teachings about the universe found in the Bible and taught by the church. When Galileo revealed his discoveries to the world, his troubles began. The Catholic church, then an all-powerful authority in matters of philosophy and science, as well as religion, had him arrested.

From his earliest years, Galileo was an original and rebellious thinker in an age when most people still believed what they were told to believe. He was born in

Galileo Galilei

1564 in Pisa, the town in Italy well known then, as it is today, for its leaning tower. Galileo was a brilliant young man. At the age of 25, he was already a professor of mathematics and science at the University of Pisa. Before he was 33, he had discovered the principle of the pendulum and the law of falling bodies. He had also found a new method for weighing objects in water to determine their specific gravity, and had invented the *sector*, a type of compass still used by draftsmen today.

By the time Galileo began teaching at the University of Padua in 1592, he was widely recognized as one of the most brilliant men in Europe. It was also at Padua, unfortunately, that his troubles began.

In 1608 Hans Lippershey, a Dutch scientist, had invented the telescope. Galileo learned of the invention, and the next year he built one himself. Galileo's telescope was much stronger than Lippershey's. When he looked through it he could see the sun, moon, stars, and planets strongly magnified. With this enlarged view, he soon discovered some very interesting facts about certain heavenly bodies. He saw things that people had never before been able to observe.

Galileo discovered that there were not 7 planets and satellites, as everyone believed in those days, but at least 11. With his telescope, he spotted 4 new satellites around the planet Jupiter. He also observed that the planet Saturn had a ring around it and that the planet Venus went through phases, waxing and waning just as the moon does. In addition, he observed "spots" on the sun — dark areas that we know today are whirling storms of gases — and hills and valleys on the surface of the moon.

From many of his observations, Galileo drew several important conclusions about the motion of the planets.

In Galileo's time, most astronomers believed that the earth was the center of the universe and that it was motionless. The sun and the other planets, they believed, revolved around the earth. The church firmly upheld these ideas.

Galileo's observations, however, led him to the opposite conclusion. He believed, correctly, that the earth moved around the sun, and not the other way around. Not only that, but he believed that the earth was spinning on its axis as well. His observations added support to the earlier theories of Nicolaus Copernicus, a famed Polish astronomer who in 1543 had published a book putting forth these radical new ideas.

In 1610, Galileo published his own ideas and discoveries in a book entitled *Sidereal Message*. (*Sidereal* means of or relating to the stars.) Almost immediately, Galileo's ideas were disputed by the Catholic church because they were different from the church's views. In arguing against Galileo's ideas, biblical scholars pointed to passages in the Bible to uphold the church's view of the universe. One critic of Galileo, for example, said that the Bible pointed out that there were "seven cardinal virtues...seven golden candlesticks in Moses...seven heavens...seven days of creation...seven plagues...." Therefore, said the scholar, there *must* be 7 planets and satellites, not 11 as Galileo had claimed.

Other members of the church said flatly that it didn't matter what Galileo was seeing in his telescope. If it was contrary to what was described in the Bible and believed by the church, then it was wrong. What Galileo was seeing, they said, must be nothing more than an illusion.

Galileo continued to argue strongly for his views. But in 1616, Pope Paul V ordered Galileo to stop teaching his

Pope Urban VIII

ideas. If Galileo did not stop, the pope informed him, he would be arrested and put in jail. Galileo agreed to go along with the church, although he still believed he was right.

Sixteen years later, however, there was a new pope, Urban VIII. He knew Galileo and was friendly toward him. Galileo requested permission from him to publish certain of his ideas in a book called *Dialogue on the Two Principal Systems of the World.* The pope agreed.

The pope, however, placed several restrictions on the book. If Galileo wanted to discuss the ideas of Copernicus, he must present them only as theory, not as fact. The pope

specified that Galileo had to write a *preface*, or introduction, to the book in which the church's ideas were
clearly stated. In addition, the book would have to be
approved, the pope said, by the Inquisitor of Florence,
a specially appointed priest in the city where Galileo was
then living.

Galileo happily set about the task of writing the book.
When he finished, he submitted it to the inquisitor, who
approved it. This enabled it to be published with the
imprimatur, the church's formal seal of approval, printed
right in the book. As later events were to prove, however,
the inquisitor did not understand what he read and
approved.

Dialogue was written in the form of various conversations among three men. Two of them were learned, and
one, named Simplicio, was an idiot. Galileo's ideas were
presented for the most part by one of the learned men,
Salviati. Opposing ideas, or those held by the church,
were for the most part presented in the words of Simplicio,
the fool, and were then torn apart by the wiser men.

Dialogue was accepted almost immediately by many
of the intellectuals of Galileo's day as a great book from
the mind of a great scientist. Many considered it to be
one of the most important books that had been written
up to that time.

Not everyone, however, shared those feelings. When the
pope read the book, he was furious. He saw many of his
own ideas, arguments, and philosophies presented in the
words of an idiot. On top of that, they were made to look
absurd by the arguments of the scholar Salviati. Galileo's
fortunes took a turn for the worse. The pope ordered the
book to be banned. Galileo was told to report immediately
to Rome and to present himself before the pope.

Formal charges were drawn up against Galileo. They were the following:

1. He had placed the imprimatur of the church on the book without proper permission from the pope in Rome.
2. He had presented the church's views only in a preface that was separated from the main body of the book, and in the words of an idiot in the main text of the book.
3. He had not treated the ideas of Copernicus as theory but had presented them as if they were fact.
4. He had treated the idea of the earth rotating on its axis and revolving around the sun as if it were a possibility, when in fact, the church had already decided that such ideas were false.
5. He had condemned those who held the opinions of the church.
6. He had held that there is equality between the human mind and the divine mind in understanding scientific and mathematical ideas.
7. He wished to convert those who agreed with the church that the earth was the center of the universe to his own beliefs.

Galileo was no longer a young man when he set out for Rome to answer the charges against him. He was 69 years old, and his health was not good. But he had to make the hard journey. As it turned out, the trip was to be the easiest part of his ordeal.

Shortly after his arrival in Rome, Galileo was put in jail. There, he was questioned by the inquisitors. These were special churchmen who investigated and tried persons suspected of heresy — the crime of holding beliefs

Before his trial, Galileo was put in prison, where he was questioned by the inquisitors.

that did not agree with those of the church. In those days, questioning by the inquisitors was often rugged, and torture was common and severe. But because of Galileo's great reputation as a scientist and because of his old age, he was assigned comfortable quarters in the jail and a servant to tend to his needs. There is no evidence that he was tortured; nevertheless, something happened to Galileo while he was in prison that changed his entire behavior.

Galileo had been told by the inquisitors that under no circumstances would he be allowed to argue *for* his ideas at the trial. His guilt or innocence — whether he was right or wrong in his thinking — was not the issue. In effect, he had already been found guilty of heresy. He stood convicted, and his trial was really being held to determine his punishment.

The court in Rome was composed of 10 cardinals of the Catholic church. They would hear the case and render the sentence. Although Galileo could not argue on behalf of his ideas at the trial, witnesses were brought in to refute them. Evidence was presented to show that Galileo had violated Pope Paul V's ruling of 1616, which had forbidden him to teach the ideas of Copernicus. Then Galileo was asked what he had to say for himself.

Somehow Galileo had changed during his imprisonment because now he tried hard to explain away all that he had written. Galileo said that he had been under the impression that he could teach the Copernican ideas if he treated them as theory only, which he had tried to do. Apparently he had failed, he said. He added that in his latest book, he had really been trying to show that the Copernican ideas were *wrong,* and that the church's teachings about the universe were correct. Apparently, he said, he had failed in that attempt as well.

It was hard to believe that the Galileo speaking at his trial was the same Galileo who had spoken so strongly before in defense of his ideas. But it was the same man.

The church, however, was still not satisfied. Authorities in Rome brought Galileo back for another trial. At this hearing, he went even further and confessed, "I do not hold, and have never held, the opinions of Copernicus since the order was given me (in 1616) to abandon them."

Galileo was then ordered to write out his full confession of guilt. He did, and was then formally pronounced guilty by the court.

The church plainly wanted to make an example of

Galileo on trial for heresy

Galileo. Church officials wanted to hold him up before the world to show what would happen to someone who went against the church's teachings.

The inquisitor's sentence for Galileo's crime had three parts. First, his book was to be banned forever. Second, he was sentenced to prison for the remainder of his life. Third, he was ordered to give a public abjuration — that is, a retraction of what he had written in his book.

In June 1633, in a convent near the center of Rome, Galileo was made to kneel and read aloud his abjuration before the 10 judges and various other witnesses. Galileo said slowly but clearly:

> I, Galileo, aged 70 years...kneeling before you...
> having before my eyes and touching with my hands
> the Holy Gospel, swear that I have always believed,

do believe, and by God's help will in the future believe all that is held, preached, and taught by the Holy Catholic and Apostolic Church....

Galileo then went on to describe his offenses:

I have been pronounced by the Holy Office to be vehemently suspected of heresy, that is to say, of having held and believed that the sun is the center of the world and immovable, and that the Earth is not the center and moves. Therefore, desiring to remove from the minds of your eminences and of all faithful Christians, this vehement suspicion justly conceived against me, with sincere heart and unfeigned faith, I abjure, curse, and detest the aforesaid errors and heresies...and I swear that in the future I will never again say or assert, verbally or in writing, anything that might furnish occasion for a similar suspicion regarding me....

And so Galileo renounced the scientific truths that he had discovered and had written about. It is said, however, that when he was rising from his knees after his public retraction, he said softly under his breath, "And yet it moves," referring, of course, to the earth.

Galileo was not forced to go to prison. Instead, he was allowed to remain at home in Florence under house arrest. He could see only his family, and he was not allowed to venture outside. He continued to write, but his eyes finally failed him and he went blind. He died at the age of 78, eight years after his abjuration.

Galileo knew that most of what he had discovered and written about was correct. Why, then, did this brilliant man deny what he knew to be true? One reason, no doubt, was to save his life, for death would surely have been the penalty if he had not renounced what he had written. Had he refused to renounce his ideas, he also would have been excommunicated, or expelled, from the church, and thus from the religion in which he ardently believed despite his scientific disagreements with the church. To Galileo, as to all devout Catholics, excommunication from the church meant an afterlife of eternal torture in hell and of permanent exclusion from God's grace.

Thus, as Galileo was later to say himself, "If the Church insists that I *deny* what I happen to *know*, then I must obey." And so he did. Yet his great work in astronomy and physics, preserved in his writings, insures his place in history as a brilliant thinker and a founder of experimental science.

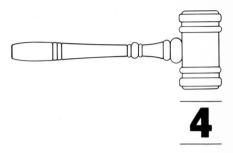

4

Captain Alfred Dreyfus

In the military, when an individual is accused of disobeying military laws or codes, he or she is brought before a *court-martial* — a special military court of law — to be tried. Usually the military's motive for trying a person is to maintain "law and order" and discipline. But in some cases, court action is brought to uphold the army's honor and good name. In the case of the French army versus Captain Alfred Dreyfus, the issue was largely one of honor. Because of the questionable circumstances in the case, this 19th-century confrontation became one of the most famous trials in history.

Alfred Dreyfus was born in 1859 in Mulhouse, in Alsace, not far from the Swiss border. He was born a Jew, a fact that was to work against him later in life. As a youth, however, he seemed destined for success. His father, a wealthy manufacturer of textiles, sent him to the best schools in France. After attending France's finest military school, Dreyfus decided to make the army his career.

Captain Alfred Dreyfus

By the age of 30, he had been promoted to the rank of captain in the French army. Five years later, in 1894, Dreyfus was serving as a staff officer in the Ministry of War in Paris. One day during that year, he was ordered to report to the Army Intelligence office. Once there, he was asked several questions, told to write something on a piece of paper, then informed that he was being placed under arrest. He was accused of betraying his nation's military secrets to another country — a crime of high treason. It was the worst crime that a soldier could commit.

Captain Dreyfus was shocked. He immediately claimed his innocence. The bewildered officer explained that he had always been loyal to France and that his record as a military officer had been spotless. His protests, however, were to no avail.

Intelligence officers said that the evidence they had against him was very strong. They had discovered a *bordereau* — a detailed memorandum — that contained an offer to turn over French military secrets to the German military attaché in Paris. The *bordereau* was signed with a D, as in Dreyfus, and the handwriting on it looked much like his. That was the extent of the evidence. This little *bordereau* was a document that would come to be known throughout the world.

The *bordereau* was real enough. It had been found at the German Embassy. And it did contain a treasonous offer. The fact of the matter was, however, that Alfred Dreyfus was not the author of it.

Unfortunately for Dreyfus, there were persons within the army who were working against him. Major Hubert Henry, the man who had questioned Dreyfus about the *bordereau,* was a good friend of the real traitor who had actually written it — Major Ferdinand Esterhazy. To protect his friend, Major Henry went along with the accusation of Dreyfus.

As for the army itself, high army officials were embarrassed by the whole incident. If word got out that one of the army's trusted officers was giving secret information to Germany, there would surely be a terrible scandal. The army wanted justice brought about quickly and the incident forgotten. It wanted *no* publicity.

It was suggested to Captain Dreyfus that he take his own life in order to avoid the damage to his reputation that a trial would bring. But he refused to commit suicide, claiming that his honor would be proven by the truth.

So the trial of Alfred Dreyfus was set for December 1894, two months after he had first been accused. Dreyfus was able to obtain the services of one of France's finest lawyers, Charles Demange.

Because the army wanted everything hushed up, it was decided that the trial would be held *in camera,* which meant that it was not to be open to the public or the press. The proceedings were to be kept absolutely secret. But somehow, news of the trial was leaked to the press. *La Libre Parole,* an anti-Semitic newspaper, eagerly printed the fact that a "Jewish traitor" was to stand trial.

The trial opened in Paris six days before Christmas, 1894. Seven judges, all high-ranking military officers, were selected to hear the case. From the very beginning of the court-martial, it was obvious to an unbiased observer that there was hardly any case against Dreyfus. The only evidence that the prosecution could present was the vague similarity between the handwriting of Dreyfus and that of the person who had written the *bordereau.* The prosecution called several witnesses — handwriting "experts" who said that the handwritings appeared to be those of the same person. There were, however, other handwriting experts called by the defense who said they were not similar at all. Years later, when the handwriting samples were finally published, it was quite clear that the two were noticeably different.

Defense lawyer Demange based much of his case on the differences in the handwritings. He also pointed out that the *bordereau* contained certain information that Dreyfus could not have even known. Therefore, he could not possibly have written the memorandum.

The case against Dreyfus was certainly weak, and high officials in the army were aware of this weakness. Yet the minister of war, General Auguste Mercier, feared that the entire army would be dishonored if Dreyfus was not found guilty. And he wanted to avoid that at all costs. Damaging information began to build up against Dreyfus. The army now found that publicity could be used to its advantage. At the trial and in the French press, it was emphasized that Dreyfus was a Jew. To many people this meant that his first allegiance was to the world community of Jews and not to any particular country. People reasoned that he was, therefore, a logical suspect in a case of treason. A *French* officer, the army wanted everyone to believe, would never commit such a terrible act.

Soon, pressure was brought to bear on the seven military judges. Witnesses from the army began to appear with strong testimony against Dreyfus. (None of it, however, was real evidence.) A secret packet of documents was also passed to the judges. In the packet were nothing more than prejudiced opinions and forged documents suggesting that Dreyfus was a traitor. The documents, the army said, could not be made public because they contained important military secrets. The defense was not allowed to examine them.

As a result, Alfred Dreyfus was found guilty of treason. He was sentenced to life imprisonment and was taken under strict guard to Devil's Island, a notorious prison island off the coast of French Guiana. The army wanted to make sure that he got no chance to talk to anyone.

Not *all* the officers in the French army, however, were convinced of Dreyfus's guilt. On the contrary, some even thought that he had been made a scapegoat and realized that he was a victim of anti-Jewish feeling.

After Dreyfus was found guilty of treason, his military sword was broken as a symbol of his disgrace.

Time passed, and some of these officers continued to investigate the case of Alfred Dreyfus. Most notable was Lieutenant Colonel Georges Picquart, chief of the army's intelligence section. His investigation pointed to Major Esterhazy as the true author of the *bordereau.* Despite attempts by the army to supress it, the evidence he uncovered resulted in charges being brought against Esterhazy and a trial being called for.

With the help of Esterhazy's old friend, Major Henry, and some other high-ranking officers in the army, however, more forged documents and false evidence were created. Witnesses lied on the stand. The result was that Esterhazy was found *not guilty.*

By this time the army found itself engaged in an extensive cover-up. The possibilities for scandal had grown worse and worse. Now the army's misdeeds included sending a man (Dreyfus) to prison on flimsy evidence, perjury in court by high-ranking army officers, withholding of evidence, forgery, and subterfuge involving many officers at the highest levels of the army. Now it was more critical than ever to keep Dreyfus in prison. Upholding the honor of the army had become much more important than the fate of one individual man.

The people of France, however, had begun to question the entire situation. Great writers and thinkers spoke out against what was going on. Among them were Anatole France, Marcel Proust, André Gide, and, most outspoken of all, writer Émile Zola.

In 1898 Zola wrote a newspaper article that bitterly denounced the trial and the sentencing of Dreyfus. Its headline — *J'accuse!* ("I accuse!") — became famous. In his article, Zola claimed that the army had actually been criminal in the way in which it had acted during the Dreyfus trial. Dreyfus, he wrote, had been denied his basic rights in court. The army had engineered a false verdict in the Dreyfus case, and it had criminally conspired in the case of Major Esterhazy as well.

The name Dreyfus was now becoming familiar throughout the world. His case had become a classic example of injustice. Alfred Dreyfus, however, sat in his prison cell on Devil's Island, knowing nothing of what was going on in his behalf.

Many people in France agreed with Émile Zola. But many officials in high places did not. Zola was arrested. The government and the army did not want to bring Zola to trial. But Zola wanted a trial, because he knew that it

51

would open up the Dreyfus case, this time for all the world to hear. The evidence for Dreyfus and the evidence against the army and the court-martial would all be brought out into the open. In this way, Zola hoped, Dreyfus would be cleared and returned to France, and justice would be done.

Zola got his wish; he was finally brought to trial. He was found guilty of committing libel against the French government and was fined and sentenced to a year in jail. But, as he had foreseen, his trial succeeded in breaking open the Dreyfus case again.

The truth began to emerge. The people of France now wanted something done about it. Major Esterhazy, sensing that the tides were turning against him, fled to England. Major Henry took more drastic action; he killed himself. The outcry for a new trial for Alfred Dreyfus grew until it had to be heeded.

Finally, in August 1899, after five years on Devil's Island, Captain Dreyfus was brought back to France for a new trial. The eyes of the world were turned upon the small town of Rennes, France, where the new court-martial was to be held.

The case had now become a direct contest between Dreyfus and the honor of the French army. And the army still had no intention of giving in. Appearing against Dreyfus was no less a figure than General Auguste Mercier, who had been minister of war when Dreyfus was originally arrested and tried. The army argued strongly that Dreyfus was guilty. The cases of Majors Esterhazy and Henry were another matter and should be disregarded, they said. The army refused to allow its honor to be discredited despite all that had been revealed in the five years since the original trial.

Although witness after witness took the stand for the

The verdict is read at Captain Dreyfus' second court-martial in 1899.

prosecution, the case against Captain Dreyfus remained woefully weak. But at the end of the five-week trial, the world was astonished to learn that the verdict had not changed! Captain Alfred Dreyfus was again found guilty.

This time, however, Dreyfus was not sent back to prison. The verdict had actually been a compromise. Dreyfus was found guilty with "extenuating circumstances." Because of this, the remainder of his sentence was cancelled. At the same time, the verdict insured that the army's honor would be kept intact. The only loser in the whole affair, of course, was Dreyfus. He escaped further imprisonment, but his honor was certainly not restored by the finding of guilty.

Alfred Dreyfus, his family, his lawyers, and all those who stood behind him refused to give up. They decided that they could not and would not tolerate the injustices that Dreyfus had experienced.

New evidence was gathered. False evidence from the past was exposed. Truths were brought out, and lies and forgeries were revealed. Finally, in 1906, an appeal to review the case was granted by France's Ministry of Justice.

The result of the appeal was to overturn the original decision. After so many years, Captain Dreyfus was finally cleared. He was also reinstated as an officer in the army. In addition, he was even awarded France's famous medal, the Legion of Honor. He went on to serve in the French army as a lieutenant colonel during World War I.

Captain Aflred Dreyfus died in 1935, leaving behind a name that will forever be associated with the miscarriage of justice and with the knowledge that injustices *can* be corrected, if only people are willing to fight against them.

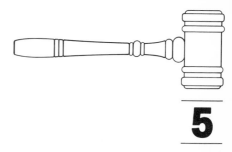

5

The Nuremberg Trials

Nuremberg is one of the oldest cities in Germany — a city of ornate stone buildings and narrow cobblestone streets, with walls and towers that date back to the Middle Ages. Located not far from the snow-capped Alps, it is a city whose history goes back almost 1,000 years.

The period before and during World War II was one of the darkest chapters in Nuremberg's long history. For it was during this time that Nuremberg was a key center of activity for the Nazi party.

The Nazi party came to power in Germany in 1933. Led by Germany's ruthless dictator, Adolf Hitler, it pursued two primary goals — the expansion of Germany and military domination of Europe, and the persecution and extermination of Jews and other minority people considered by the party to be "inferior" to the Teutonic people of Germany. From Nuremberg the Nazis issued the dreadful "Nuremberg Decrees" — edicts that prescribed the grim destiny of the Jewish people under the Third Reich.

Jews in the Polish city of Warsaw being deported to a concentration camp

Germany began World War II in 1939, when Hitler's armies invaded Poland. The Germans moved on through Belgium, the Netherlands, Luxembourg, Norway, Denmark, France, and finally the Soviet Union.

All during this period of attack and conquest, the Nazi party operated a systematic program of persecution against the Jews of Europe. The party confiscated the homes and property of the Jews, separated thousands of families, and confined men, women, and children to the horrors of the concentration camps, where they were treated with incredible brutality and where millions were eventually put to death.

Fighting the Nazi war machine were the Allied forces of the United States, Britain, France, and Russia, as well as the armies of many European nations. Midway through

1944, the war finally turned decisively against the Germans. Allied forces from the United States, Britain, and Canada landed in France on D-Day, June 6, to stop the German advance across France. Other Allied forces were fighting their way up toward Germany through Italy. And Soviet forces were crushing in from the east.

By April 1945, Germany was on the verge of collapse. Adolf Hitler committed suicide only days before Germany surrendered to the Allies in May 1945.

All that remained was the rubble of a six-year war, the worst in the world's history. Entire cities were destroyed. Millions of people, soldiers, and civilians alike, were dead. In the aftermath of the war, the Allied troops found relics of the German concentration camps — the few starving survivors, the huge graves where thousands had been shot and dumped, the gas chambers where millions had died, and the monstrous ovens where bodies had been disposed of. All these were grim evidence of some of the

Prisoners in the concentration camp of Dachau welcome American troops at the end of the war.

worst crimes ever committed in human history.

So terrible was the devastation that when the war was over, the Allied governments — the United States, England, France, and the Soviet Union — announced that they would bring to trial all the persons and organizations responsible for starting the war and for persecuting the Jews and other minority peoples.

Representatives of the four nations gathered together in England to define the course they would take. Out of their talks came what was to be known as the London Agreement of August 8, 1945.

The agreement stated that the four major Allies would act on behalf of all the countries that had been at war with Germany. The Allies established an International Military Tribunal whose authority and validity could not be challenged by either the prosecutors (the Allies) or the defendants (the German war criminals). The agreement also outlined in detail the way in which the Tribunal would be set up — what judges, attorneys, and other officials would participate, as well as what procedures would be followed during the trials.

The site for the trials was Nuremberg. The city had been practically leveled by the massive bombings of the American and British air forces, but the huge building that housed the palace of justice and the prison was still standing. It was selected as the place where the trials of the highest-ranking German war criminals would be held. Thus the proceedings came to be known as the "Nuremberg trials."

The defendants — those accused of war crimes — were numerous. Of course, the highest-ranking war criminal, Adolf Hitler, was dead. So were a number of other high-ranking Germans, including Joseph Goebbels, chief of propaganda and one of the three most powerful men in Germany, and Heinrich Himmler, top man in the dreaded SS (Hitler's private police guard), who among other things had planned and administrated the concentration camps.

There were, however, plenty of other top-ranking Nazis who had been captured. The Allies agreed to bring charges against 24 of them as well as against six Nazi organizations.

But there was no true precedent for the kind of trials that the Allies were planning. Before Nuremberg, there were no rules defining a war crime, or specifying who could be charged and tried for committing such a crime. Throughout history, nations have had rules of warfare and have conducted trials of persons or groups that violated these rules. But these had been scattered trials, usually conducted only at the whim of the victors. From the trials at Nuremberg was to come the first real international definition of what constituted a war crime. Three broad and major Articles of Indictment were laid down. These were:

1. *Crimes Against Peace.* These included the planning, initiating, and/or waging of a war of aggression — a war in violation of international treaties, agreements or assurances, and participation in a common plan or conspiracy for waging such a war.

2. *Conventional War Crimes.* These included violations of the laws or customs governing war. Such violations were murder, ill-treatment, or deportation of the civilian population of occupied territory; murder or ill-treatment of prisoners of war or persons on the seas; killing of hostages; plunder of public or private property; and wanton destruction of cities, towns, or villages — that is, destruction not justified by military necessity.

3. *Crimes Against Humanity.* These included murder, extermination, enslavement, deportation, and other inhumane acts committed against any civilian population, either before or during a war; and persecution of people on political, racial, or religious grounds during the execution of, or in connection with, any other war crime.

The charges were now defined. The list of those to be tried was agreed upon; the charges were brought against 24 defendants. No one would dispute that these 24 had earned their places on the roster of war criminals.

First on the list of those Nazis still alive was Hermann

Göring. As *Reichsmarschall,* he had been the second-highest ranking Nazi after Hitler himself. He had been a major participant in practically every important decision made by Hitler. He had controlled the German economy, had been chief of the *Luftwaffe* (the German air force), and had founded the *Gestapo,* the dreaded Nazi secret police.

Göring had also played a major role in developing plans to exterminate the Jewish people. And he had sanctioned and participated in the plundering of vast riches of art from various countries, much of which he kept for himself in his mansion *Karinhall.* There was very little that had gone on in the Third Reich with which Hermann Göring had not been associated.

Next in the line of power was Martin Bormann. Bormann had been Hitler's secretary, and the power of his office had been enormous. He was one of the two or three most powerful men in Germany at the end of the war. Bormann was known as an ardent "Jew-hater" and was closely involved with creating and carrying out the extermination program. Unfortunately, he had never been captured. Some said that he had been killed in the last days of the war. Others said he had escaped and was at large somewhere, trying to make his way to South America. In either event, he would not be present at his trial and would, therefore, be tried *in absentia.*

Joachim von Ribbentrop had been Germany's foreign minister, a position equal to that of the United States's secretary of state. Ribbentrop was among the most hated men in German politics, often as much despised by his colleagues in the Reich as by the Allies. This arrogant man had participated closely in Germany's original plans to wage war against the rest of Europe. He was also linked criminally with the mistreatment of prisoners of war, with enforcing slave labor, and with the development of the concentration camps.

The case of Rudolf Hess was a strange one. He had held an important position as Hitler's deputy early in the war. But one day in 1941, he had stolen an airplane and flown to England because, for some strange reason, he believed he could talk England into joining forces with Germany and ending the war. He was thought by everyone to be insane and had spent the remainder of the war in an English prison. In his earlier days, however, he had held a very high position in the decision-making apparatus of the Third Reich. So he was included among the defendants at Nuremberg.

Also included was Alfred Rosenberg, who had formulated the doctrine on which nazism was based. He had also contributed substantially to the overall program for treatment of the Jews and other minorities.

From the German army, there were the two highest-ranking officers — Field Marshal Wilhelm Keitel and General Alfred Jodl, both of whom had directed and carried out the aggressive war of attack dictated by Hitler.

From the German navy were two top admirals — Karl Dönitz and Erich Raeder, both of whom were deeply involved in the Third Reich's military plans.

Other defendants were Ernst Kaltenbrunner, the highest-ranking SS officer; Julius Streicher and Fritz Sauckel, both responsible for many acts of brutality against the Jews; Albert Speer, who had kept the Nazis supplied with arms and munitions; and Baldur von Schirach, the director of the Nazi party's youth program, which indoctrinated the youth against the Jews and trained them for military action.

Professional men, businessmen, and men in public life were also charged with crimes. Hans Frank, Hitler's personal lawyer, had become governor of Poland and had allowed more than a million Polish Jews to be murdered. Hjalmer Schacht and Walther Funk had often used illegal means to handle the Third Reich's finances, and Hans Fritzsche, head of German broadcasting, had used his communication network to spread Nazi propaganda. Artur Seyss-Inquart, whom Hitler appointed to govern the Netherlands, allowed many crimes to be committed against the Dutch people, especially the Jews. Wilhelm Frick, Hitler's minister of the interior, also committed many crimes against the Jewish people. And Constantin von Neurath and Franz von Papen, both diplomats for Hitler, supported the dictator's military and political efforts.

Also indicted was industrialist Gustav Krupp. He was the head of the family that for many years had run the Krupp Works, the huge manufacturing complex that specialized in producing arms and munitions. Krupp, however, was an old and very ill man. He was indicted at Nuremberg, but because of his failing health he was not forced to stand trial.

Robert Ley, chief of the Third Reich's labor front, would not stand trial either. He had been charged with many crimes against humanity, but had poisoned himself while in prison and had died before he could be brought to trial.

Of the 24, therefore, only 21 would stand trial. Ley was dead. Krupp was too ill. And Martin Bormann, or his dead body, was nowhere to be found.

The 21 defendants were held in the Nuremberg prison under the tightest security. Having seen what many of the high-ranking Nazis had done to avoid the trials, the

Soldiers guarding the accused war criminals in Nuremberg prison

Allies had guards watch each prisoner 24 hours a day. The Allies did not want anyone to escape trial by committing suicide.

Meanwhile, the trials were being set up and organized according to the special rules and procedures developed in the Allies' London Agreement. It was decided that all the defendants would be tried together in one major session of the court. Each, however, would be prosecuted and sentenced separately for his individual crimes.

The cases would be heard by four appointed judges. (Four alternate judges would also sit in at the trials in the event that something happened to one of the primary judges.) Each of the four major Allies — the United States, Britain, France, and the Soviet Union — would provide one judge and one alternate judge.

The judge representing Britain, Lord Justice Geoffrey Lawrence, was named president and presiding judge of the Tribunal. The other three primary judges were Francis Biddle, the attorney general of the United States, Professor Henri Donnedieu de Vabres of France, and Major General I.T. Nikitichenko of the Soviet Union.

The prosecution consisted of four principal lawyers from the four Allied countries. Each would present a particular case for his country as well as specific aspects of the general Allied case against the war criminals.

The prosecutor from the United States was Robert H. Jackson, a justice of the United States Supreme Court. It was his task to present the prosecution's opening statement, defining all charges against the defendants and laying the foundation for the trial. In addition, he was responsible for presenting the case for conspiracy on the part of the defendants to wage an aggressive and illegal war.

Sir Hartley Shawcross, the attorney general and top prosecutor in England, was to prove the charges outlined under the first Article of Indictment — "Crimes Against Peace."

The chief prosecutor of France, François de Menthon, would present the Allies' charges of crimes outlined in the second and third articles — "Conventional War Crimes" and "Crimes Against Humanity."

The difficult task of summarizing and reviewing *all* the charges and presenting them to the court after all testimony was concluded fell to the Soviet Union's leading prosecutor, General R. A. Rudenko.

The Allies also drew up a list of German lawyers for the defendants to choose from. The defendants were not, however, restricted to the list and could select any lawyer they wanted. Each defendant was to have his own personal lawyer to argue his case.

On October 18, 1945, the three Articles of Indictment were publicly read in Berlin. Under the three articles, the specific crimes were named. They included:

> ...the extermination of 5,700,000 Jews...murders of millions of Russians, Poles, Gypsies...persecution of priests, clergy...importation of six million men and women as slave labor...ghastly medical experiments on human beings...frauds...deceits...torture...conspiracy to wage aggressive war...violation of international treaties...ruthless disregard of the laws of humanity....

The Nuremberg trials did not truly get under way until November 20, 1945, when they officially opened in Nuremberg. On that day, all 21 defendants stood before the Tribunal and offered their plea — *not guilty.*

The next day, Justice Jackson of the United States gave the opening statement for the prosecution. In it, he echoed the feelings of all the Allies in regard to the defendants before them. He said:

> We will show them to be the living symbols of racial hatred, of terrorism and violence, and of the arrogance and cruelty of power. They are symbols of fierce nationalism and militarism, of intrigue and warmaking which have embroiled Europe generation after generation, crushing its manhood, destroying its homes, and impoverishing its life....

The four judges and their alternates take their places at the Nuremburg trial.

During the long trial, which was to last more than 10 months, security was as tight in the courtroom as it was in the prison. The defendants were brought in one at a time. They were thoroughly searched before each session. Their lawyers were also searched before they were allowed into the courtroom.

The four prosecutors had a gigantic case to present. The evidence was vast; there were volumes of testimony and endless statements and documentary evidence. But piece by piece, the prosecution built its case and placed it before the four judges of the Tribunal. At the end of the trial, the transcripts of what had gone on in court totalled more than a million pages. The number of documents and papers presented as evidence was so enormous that whole teams of lawyers were required just to sort them out. The "paper" evidence in regard to the SS alone filled six railroad freight cars.

The reason that there was such a tremendous amount of documentary evidence was that the Allies had been surprisingly successful in capturing huge storehouses of records and documents regarding the activities of the Third Reich. Usually a nation at war would not have left these for the conquering countries to find. But somehow, during the last days before the surrender, the Nazis did not get around to destroying all of their sensitive records.

The crimes committed by the Germans of the Third Reich were well known. The evidence against the defendants was certainly there, tons upon tons of it. At first glance, therefore, the Nuremberg trials would appear to be a simple, uncomplicated matter. Yet to this day the trials remain controversial. The reason for this is twofold. First, many people question the fairness of the trials. Second, many experts feel that the trials had no firm basis in international law.

The first concern — the fairness of the trials — is in question on several points. For one thing, it was a fact that the defense lawyers and the prosecutors were not treated equally. The defense lawyers were denied access to Allied war records; the prosecutors were not. The defense lawyers were given only one month to prepare their cases (not much time in view of the enormous amount of evidence involved), while the prosecutors had much more time to prepare their case. In addition, the Allied authorities often did little to cooperate with the defense lawyers. In one instance, a defense lawyer returning after a lunch break to continue his cross-examination of a witness was not let back into the courtroom by the American guards for more than an hour after court was back in session. The most important question, however, was whether it was at all possible for the defendants to get a fair trial at the hands of their conquerors, the same people who had been their sworn enemies at war only months earlier.

On the other hand, it was said at the trial that the Allies provided far fairer treatment of the defendants than the defendants had afforded to the millions that they had murdered. While this is undeniably true, it is not *legal* justification for holding the trials.

The second question — whether the trials were authorized under international law in the first place — was also based on several points.

One concern was that the crimes were *ex post facto,* that is, "after the fact." This meant that the defendants were being tried for acts which had *not* been crimes in their country when they were actually committed. At that time, the acts had been legal in Germany. Therefore, in the strictly legal sense, the defendants had not committed crimes.

Critics also asked whether a person could be tried for having carried out a lawful order of his or her government, even if that order was obviously immoral. This was an important point, because almost to the man, the defendants at Nuremberg explained in their defense that they were only carrying out the policies of their government and the orders of their superiors. This placed the ultimate responsibility for the crimes in the hands of the dictator, Adolf Hitler, who, of course, could not be tried.

The court at Nuremberg, however, did not accept this line of reasoning as a defense. And in disagreeing, the Tribunal set down a very important legal precedent. In

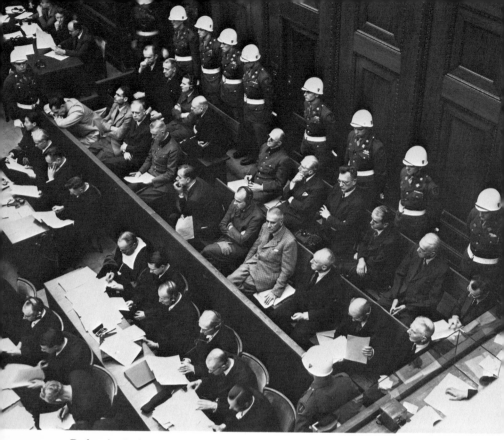

Defendants in the Nuremberg war crimes trial: *(front row, left to right)* Hermann Göring, Rudolf Hess, Joachim von Ribbentrop, Wilhelm Keitel, Alfred Rosenberg, Hans Frank, Wilhelm Frick, Julius Streicher, Walther Funk, Hjalmar Schacht; *(back row, left to right)* Karl Dönitz, Erich Raeder, Baldur von Schirach, Fritz Sauckel, Alfred Jodl, Franz von Papen, Artur Seyss-Inquart, Albert Speer, Constantin von Neurath, Hans Fritzsche. Another defendant, Ernst Kaltenbrunner, was in the hospital at the time this picture was taken.

effect, the Tribunal said that crimes of such obvious cold-bloodedness and immorality — mass murder, for example — could not be excused either as a result of carrying out lawful orders or by reason of the fact that the acts were not illegal in a particular country at a particular time. Every person, the Tribunal said, had a responsibility in such a situation to act in a proper way and to uphold the basic standards of humanity and morality. If a person chose to go along with inhumane acts, he or she could be considered as guilty as the person who had given the orders to perform such acts.

The major trial at Nuremberg finally ended in late September 1946. The four judges retired to their chambers for two days to reach their verdicts.

In their decisions, 3 of the defendants — Franz von Papen, Hjalmar Schacht, and Hans Fritzsche — were acquitted. The other 19 were found guilty and sentenced. Twelve of them, including Göring and the absent Bormann, received the death sentence. Hess, Raeder, Funk, and Dönitz were sentenced to life imprisonment. Speer, von Schirach, and von Neurath received lesser prison sentences.

Those defendants sentenced to death were hanged on October 16, 1946. The only exception was Hermann Göring, who poisoned himself with a cyanide capsule that had been smuggled to him on the day appointed for his execution. The others went to prison to serve their terms.

This trial at Nuremberg was only the beginning of a series of trials of war criminals from World War II. In all, about 200 leaders of the Third Reich were brought to trial from 1945 until 1949.

Although the controversy over the legality of the Nuremberg trials still goes on, no one can deny the brutality of the crimes committed by these men against their fellow human beings in those dark days, not so very long ago.

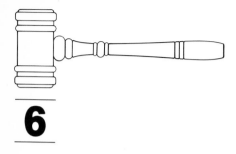

6

Cardinal Joseph Mindszenty

When World War II ended in Europe, it was soon followed by a *Cold War* between two *blocs,* or groups, of nations — the Communist countries, and those nations with democratic governments. During World War II the two groups had been *allies,* or partners, in the fight against Nazi Germany. Together, the Soviet Union, France, Britain, and the United States had succeeded in defeating the Germans, who surrendered in May 1945. The following July, the victorious Allied leaders met at Potsdam, Germany, to work out a plan for rebuilding and reorganizing postwar Europe. It was at Potsdam that trouble among the Allies began. The Communist government of the Soviet Union was moving toward control of a number of eastern European countries — Hungary, Czechoslovakia, Poland, Bulgaria, Rumania, Yugoslavia, Albania, East Germany, and the Baltic nations. The Soviets' plan was to create one large, unified bloc of Communist nations in eastern Europe. The nations of the *free* world — the democratic nations — opposed such goals. The relationship between the two sides grew more and more bitter and competitive, and people began to use the term *Cold War* to describe the struggle for political power that was going on between them.

Between 1945 and 1947, an invisible barrier was raised between the Communist bloc nations and the rest of Europe. This barrier, which came to be known as the *iron curtain,* separated the two sides in the Cold War just as a battle line would separate nations in a "hot" war.

The nations on the eastern side of the iron curtain had to learn to adjust to the Soviet Union's communist philosophy and way of life. Under communism, all land, natural resources, business, industry, and mass communications were, in theory, owned collectively by the people. In practice, however, the government controlled the political policies and economy through the Communist party, the only party with any real power. The Soviet Communists believed for the most part that the state and the Party's goals were more important than an individual's rights and wishes and that people should put allegiance to the Party above any other commitment. For this reason, the Soviets did not allow the traditional religions and their churches to function freely. They believed that religion distracted people from their duties and their allegiance to the state.

All of these new ideas and ways of life were strange to the people of Hungary, Yugoslavia, and other eastern European nations that fell under Soviet Communist control. As might be expected, the new way of life was not easily accepted by everyone. The tragic case of Cardinal Joseph Mindszenty demonstrates what happened to some of those who tried to resist.

Cardinal Joseph Mindszenty *(center)* attended a solemn mass at New York's St. Patrick's Cathedral in July 1947. In this picture, he is accompanied by Cardinal Francis Spellman of New York *(right)* and Archbishop James Duhig of Brisbane, Australia *(left)*.

Joseph Mindszenty had been appointed Roman Catholic cardinal of Hungary in 1945 by Pope Pius XII. His life was devoted to God and to the Catholic church, and he feared for the freedom of his church under his nation's new regime. Cardinal Mindszenty protested openly against what was happening in Hungary under the Communist government.

Because of Mindszenty's position as leader of all Roman Catholics in that country, Hungarian government officials were worried. They knew that Mindszenty had the power to influence a great many people. They kept him under close surveillance for a while, and they made frequent attempts to persuade him to go along with the changes that they were trying to bring about. The cardinal, however, could not be budged.

By 1948, the Communist movement was well under way in Hungary. The Hungarian Communist government confiscated the properties of the church during that year and also took direct control of the church's schools. In effect, the government made the church a subject of the state.

Cardinal Mindszenty continued to protest, but soon his voice was not to be heard anywhere in Hungary.

On the day after Christmas 1948, a large convoy of Hungarian police cars pulled up in front of the cardinal's home in the Hungarian capital of Budapest. As some of the policemen moved into the street and surrounded the building, others rushed inside. There they seized the cardinal. They told him he was under arrest for the crime of high treason against the nation of Hungary.

Mindszenty was taken outside, pushed into the back of a large police van, and taken to the Andrassy Street prison and interrogation center. At the prison, which was known and feared by people throughout Budapest, Cardinal Mindszenty was stripped of his religious clothing and informed that he was now nothing more than a simple citizen of the state. He was also told of what crimes against the state he now stood accused. He was informed that he had conspired against the state by the following actions:

1. his protest to the Hungarian premier against the founding of a Communist republic in Hungary;
2. his contacts with the exiled former archduke of Hungary, Otto Hapsburg, an enemy of the state, in regard to overthrowing the Communist government;

3. his alleged creation of a list of cabinet officers who were to take charge when the Communists were overthrown in Hungary;
4. his attempts to stir up trouble between the United States and Hungary, in order to provoke a war.

The cardinal had made it clear to the world that he believed in the supremacy of the church over the state. His protests had been loud and bitter — until he visited Andrassy Street. That was the beginning of the ordeal of Cardinal Joseph Mindszenty. No one except Mindszenty and his interrogators knows for sure all that went on behind the walls of the Andrassy Street prison. But when Mindszenty emerged from prison to stand trial a little more than a month after his arrest, he was a very changed man.

Some facts are known about his ordeal. It is known that he was questioned almost constantly. On one occasion, in fact, he was interrogated without interruption for more than three days and three nights until he finally collapsed. Later the cardinal himself, as well as eyewitnesses, told of many beatings inflicted on him with a rubber hose. The cardinal also claimed that drugs were used on him. And he was the victim, he said, of a well-planned and systematic form of torture now known as *brainwashing*. He said, "My powers of resistance gradually faded....I became insecure in my judgment. Day and night my alleged sins had been hammered into me, and now I myself began to think that somehow I might very well be guilty."

Cardinal Mindszenty appeared in court on February 3, 1949. He looked like a man who had undergone severe stress. He was tense, and his arms were tightly folded

Cardinal Mindszenty *(left)* confers with a lawyer at his trial in February 1949.

across his chest. His once-strong eyes shown a deep-rooted fear, and they moved quickly from object to object. Those who had known him before he had entered the Andrassy Street prison barely recognized him now as he stood before the court.

While Mindszenty had been in prison, his case had become the topic of international concern. The Cold War was well entrenched, and there was strong hostility between the Communist countries and the free world. The free world claimed that Cardinal Mindszenty was a martyr, that he was being unjustly tried on trumped-up charges simply because he would not accept Communist doctrines. The Communist countries, on the other hand, said that Mindszenty was simply a man who had willfully and knowingly committed high treason. He had been caught and was now to be tried for the crime of attempting to overthrow the Communist government in Hungary.

The court that tried Mindszenty was composed of a judge, or "president" as he was called in Hungary, and a jury. The president himself did much of the prosecuting and questioning. There was also a prosecutor who asked those questions not asked by the president, and who presented the state's case. Cardinal Mindszenty was allowed to select his own defense lawyer, but only after many of his first choices were turned down by the government.

The defense, however, mattered very little. Once the indictment had been read, the prosecution introduced as evidence a letter of confession allegedly written in prison by Cardinal Mindszenty. In it, he had supposedly written, "I voluntarily admit that I have committed the acts I am charged with according to the penal code of the state."

Mindszenty was not permitted to say anything at the trial about the letter's authenticity or about how it had been obtained. Later, however, he said, "...the police composed this letter, not I. The handwritten version...was a forgery."

The trial proceeded along these lines. The president questioned witnesses against Mindszenty. Documents and letters supposedly written by the cardinal were introduced to show that he had conspired to commit treason. Mindszenty himself was questioned, but he was allowed to testify only on those points that the prosecutor specifically asked him. And his thinking and responses were hindered considerably by the sad state of his physical and mental health.

The defense did not have much of a chance. The way

in which the trial was set up permitted no witnesses to be introduced on behalf of the defense. Nor could the defense cross-examine witnesses for the prosecution. In two days, the trial was over.

On the third day, the prosecution and the defense summed up their cases. The prosecution demanded a guilty verdict and a sentence of death. The defense simply asked for mercy because Mindszenty had "confessed his guilt." Not surprisingly, Cardinal Joseph Mindszenty was found guilty. Then the tired and tormented man was informed that his sentence was life imprisonment. He was immediately taken away to a prison, the name and location of which was kept secret. There, he was placed in solitary confinement. He was to see no one but his guards.

When the verdict and sentence were announced, there were cries of injustice from many parts of the globe. The Vatican, the United States, England, and Canada were among those who protested. But there was nothing that they could do besides voice their opinions.

Mindszenty appealed his case, requesting that the verdict be dismissed. The prosecution appealed, too, asking that the sentence be changed to death as had originally been demanded. Six months after the trial, the appeals on both sides were denied. The treason trial of Cardinal Joseph Mindszenty was formally over. But the cardinal was to be heard from again.

In November 1956, many people in Hungary rose up against the Communist government. The "freedom fighters," as the rebels were called, succeeded in overthrowing the government. They freed Cardinal Mindszenty from his solitary confinement cell, thus enabling him to see his country free of Communist domination. But this freedom was to last only a few short days. The Soviet

Cardinal Mindszenty with some of the Hungarian freedom fighters who released him from solitary confinement in November 1956

Union immediately sent in a large force of tanks and troops too powerful for the Hungarian freedom fighters to combat. Once again the country fell back into Communist hands. Cardinal Mindszenty fled to the American Embassy in Budapest, where he was granted asylum.

Inside the embassy, Mindszenty was safe from his enemies. But if he set foot outside it, he was immediately subject to arrest again. In a sense he was still in prison, although it was a confinement far different from that which he had experienced during the preceding eight years.

Mindszenty remained in the American Embassy for 15 years. During that time, the Cold War lost its intensity and the iron curtain was raised, at least partially. Finally, in 1971, the Hungarian government made an agreement with the Vatican to allow Cardinal Mindszenty to leave the country. After 23 long years, he was at last a free man. He went into exile in Rome and finally settled in Vienna, Austria, where he died in 1975. There are still many questions that have never been fully answered regarding the case of Cardinal Joseph Mindszenty. What was his role behind the scenes in Hungary before he was arrested? Was he truly urging an overthrow of the government? And what, exactly, happened to him at the Andrassy Street prison? These questions may never be answered.

There is no question at all, however, that he was the victim of a harsh and oppressive form of government. His trial was really nothing more than an open-and-shut exercise in accusation and punishment — a trial more appropriate in the cruel days of the Middle Ages than in the supposedly civilized world of the 20th century.

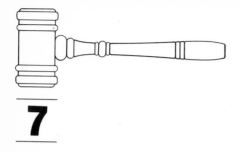

7

Adolf Eichmann

One May evening in 1960 in Buenos Aires, Argentina, a slender man with dark-rimmed glasses stepped from a bus. The man, Ricardo Klement, was on his way home from his job at the local Mercedes-Benz automobile manufacturing plant. Suddenly two men grabbed him and forced him into a black car waiting at the curb. Klement demanded to know what they wanted. But privately, he already knew. For years he had anticipated and feared this moment. For his real name was not Ricardo Klement— it was Adolf Eichmann. As an SS officer in Nazi Germany during World War II, he had been directly in charge of carrying out Hitler's plan for the total extermination of the Jewish people. Accused of the systematic murder of approximately six million human beings, he was one of the most wanted war criminals in the world.

His captors on that May night were agents of the nation of Israel. They and their colleagues had been trying to track him down for 14 years, and now, at last, they had him. They sent a cablegram in code to David Ben-Gurion, the prime minister of Israel. It said, "The beast is in chains...." But the agents' job was not finished — they had to get him out of Argentina. And they had a plan.

The agents held Eichmann secretly in Buenos Aires for more than a week. Then a large commercial airplane arrived from Israel. In the dark of night Eichmann was taken on board, and the plane roared off on its way back to the city of Tel Aviv, Israel.

On May 23, 1960, Prime Minister Ben-Gurion announced to the world that Adolf Eichmann had finally been found and arrested. He announced that Eichmann would now be tried for his enormous crimes by the very people he had tried to destroy.

When they heard the news, many people and governments complained about the way in which Eichmann had been captured. They said that he had been kidnapped — taken illegally out of the country where he had been living. The government of Argentina made a formal protest, which was taken all the way to the Security Council of the United Nations. The U.N. formally reprimanded Israel for its action, but that was all. Eichmann remained in custody in Israel, and it was generally accepted that that was where he was to be tried for his crimes.

Adolf Eichmann had tried to escape from Germany in 1945, during the last days of World War II. He knew that because of the nature of his "work," he would be greatly sought-after by both the conquering forces and the Jewish people, whom he had tried to destroy. While trying to escape, he was picked up by American troops and questioned. He gave them a false name and claimed that he was only a corporal in the *Luftwaffe*, the German air force. (In fact, he was wearing a corporal's uniform at the time.)

No one ever discovered his true identity, and he was eventually placed in a prisoner of war camp in Germany. It seemed for a while that he would escape notice.

In January 1946, however, something happened to endanger his temporary "safety." During the investigations surrounding the Nuremberg war crimes trials, one of the defendants, an officer in the SS (Hitler's private police guard), gave evidence that Eichmann had been directly involved in murdering huge numbers of Jewish people. Eichmann, he said, "...had special authority...[and] was responsible for the so-called solution of the Jewish problem in Germany and all the occupied countries....It was what was called the 'final solution,' in other words, the systematic extermination of the Jewish people." Eichmann, he claimed, was the man who had actually had the Jews removed from their homes and deported to the concentration camps. Eichmann had also controlled what awaited the Jews at their destination — the gas chambers and the firing squads of the terrible death camps like Auschwitz, Dachau, Buchenwald, and the others. Eichmann, said the SS officer, was *directly* responsible for the fate of the Jews sent to these camps.

The officer also testified that Adolf Eichmann had said publicly, "I will jump into my grave laughing, extraordinarily pleased that I have the death of five million Jews on my conscience."

The world was shocked, and the search for Eichmann was intensified. Eichmann knew that he would eventually be recognized. He made a desperate attempt to escape from the prison camp, and he was successful.

For the next three years, Eichmann hid in Germany. The search for him went on but he was not discovered. Still, he knew he might be found at any time. Finally,

Hungarian Jews boarding a train bound for a concentration camp. For most, the train ride would be their last.

in 1950, Eichmann decided that the safest place for him to live was Argentina. Many other Nazi exiles were living there in relative safety. So Eichmann went to Italy, where, with the help of some Catholic priests, he obtained false identity papers and a ticket to board a ship bound for South America. He settled in Buenos Aires and later sent for his wife and three children, who came to live with him there. Eichmann worked at a series of small, unimportant jobs in Buenos Aires. He lived a rather poor life during those years, especially compared to the comfortable life he had known as a high-ranking SS officer in Germany.

As the 1950s drew to a close, practically the only agents still involved in tracking down Eichmann were the Israelis. Almost every other country had given up the search for war criminals by then. For one thing, 15 years had passed since the war had ended. And even if Eichmann were captured, there was no established court in which to try him for his crimes. The Nuremberg trials were now formally over. There was no such thing as an international court of the United Nations. The Allies — the United States, England, France, and the Soviet Union — did not appear willing to press charges at that point. And the German government seemed reluctant to bring back bitter memories of World War II by staging such a trial. There was no other country left to do the job except Israel, a nation that had not even been in existence when Eichmann's crimes were committed. Yet Israel was now the home of many survivors of the camps, and of the families and friends of those whom Eichmann had sent to their deaths. It seemed appropriate to many that Eichmann should be tried in Israel. At any rate, the Israelis had their man, and they proceeded with plans for his trial. They wanted no one to forget what had occurred in Germany under the Nazi leaders. So when they drew up their plans, they made sure that Eichmann's trial would be seen and heard throughout the world.

The preparations for the trial were so elaborate that they took 11 months to complete. Many security precautions were taken. A special bullet proof glass booth was constructed in the courtroom for Eichmann. Since the trial itself was to be conducted in Hebrew, the ancient language of the Jewish people, speakers and earphones had to be installed so that immediate translations into German could be made for Eichmann and his lawyers. In addition, it was agreed that the entire trial would be televised, so that people throughout the world could watch and listen. Thus, the courtroom was set up to accommodate cameras, lights, and sound equipment.

While these preparations were being made, Adolf Eichmann waited in a heavily guarded prison in Tel Aviv. The security around him was the tightest possible; he was watched by guards every moment of the day and night. There were several reasons for this. First, his captors feared that, like other imprisoned Nazi leaders in the past, Eichmann might try to kill himself to escape standing trial. No one could forget that, despite the tight security at Nuremberg, Nazi war criminal Hermann Göring had managed to obtain and take poison the day he was to be hanged. The Israelis were not going to let this happen with Eichmann. His food was tested by guards before it was given to him. There was *nothing* in his cell that could be used to aid him in committing suicide. The two guards who were constantly with him carried no weapons that could be taken and used by the prisoner. Instead, they were highly skilled in judo and other arts of weaponless self-defense.

The Israelis were also concerned about the people whose lives had been directly affected by Eichmann — those who had lived through the horror of the concentration camps, and those whose families and friends had been murdered. Given the opportunity, any one of these people might try to kill Eichmann on the spot. There was also evidence that Nazi officers still in exile wanted Eichmann dead so that he could not give the authorities information about them. So every precaution was taken to keep Eichmann alive.

The only time that Eichmann left his cell was when he was taken to his daily interrogation. In the beginning, he did not cooperate with the authorities who were questioning him. He doubted that they had much real evidence against him because during his years in Nazi Germany he had tried to keep his anonymity, making every effort to remain in the background and to avoid any publicity about his actions. He had never had his picture taken, except for official Gestapo or SS purposes, and when he did, he had seen to it personally that the negatives were destroyed. He had tried, in many ways, to be the "silent" minister of death. But he had not been silent enough, as he soon found out. The Israelis had gathered a vast amount of documented evidence and a long parade of witnesses who had already testified as to Eichmann's part in the "final solution." There were many others who stood ready to testify, too.

When Eichmann learned of all this, he knew his situation was relatively hopeless. And he appeared to have at least a partial change of heart. At this point during the questioning, the interrogator said to him, "I am told that you have expressed your readiness, and even an interest in giving your version of your part in the so-called Third Reich. Is this so?"

"It is so," Eichmann said.

Now, Eichmann was eager to talk. He tried to explain that his part in the vast and terrible crimes committed by the Nazis had been only to carry out orders given by his superiors. He argued that he should not be held responsible for his actions. He knew, however, that he would be held responsible nonetheless.

I was told that I should face the Court within this year, and I was told I should not survive my 56th birthday....This knowledge alone makes me absolutely ready to say everything I know without any regard for my own person....I was used to...unconditional obedience....Disobedience would in any case have been of no avail.... Those who planned, decided, directed, and ordered the things have escaped their responsibility.... Although there is no blood on my hands, I shall certainly be found guilty of participation in murder. Be that as it may, I am inwardly ready to expiate for the dark events and I know the death penalty awaits me. I do not ask for mercy because I am not entitled to it. Should it serve as a greater act of expiation, I would even be prepared to hang myself in public as a deterrent example for anti-Semites of all the countries on earth.

Later at the trial, however, he was to change his attitude considerably.

The trial of Adolf Eichmann officially began on April 11, 1961 — exactly 11 months after Eichmann had been captured in Buenos Aires. The court was composed of three judges. Presiding was the most famous jurist in Israel, Supreme Court Judge Moshe Landau. The other two judges were Dr. Benjamin Halevy, the top-ranking district court judge in Jerusalem, and Dr. Yitzhak Raveh, head of the Tel Aviv district court.

The prosecutor in the case was Israel's attorney general, Gideon Hausner. Eichmann had selected as his lawyer Dr. Robert Servatius of Cologne, Germany. Dr. Servatius was a well-known specialist in war crimes trials and had defended Fritz Sauckel, the Nazi commissioner of labor, at the Nuremberg trials 15 years earlier. The cost of Dr. Servatius's services, it was agreed, was to be paid by the government of Israel.

The charges, which were drawn up by prosecutor Gideon Hausner, were vast and legally complex. Hausner, however, later explained them simply and briefly in *Justice in Jerusalem,* a book he wrote about the Eichmann trial.

The entrance to the camp of Dachau, located 10 miles from Munich, Germany. Opened in 1933, Dachau was the Nazis' first concentration camp.

He wrote:

The first charge dealt with the ultimate murder of millions of Jews; the second, with placing them, before they were killed, in living conditions calculated to bring about their physical destruction; the third with causing them grave physical and mental harm; the fourth with devising measures for the sterilization of Jews and the prevention of childbirth among them; the fifth with causing their enslavement, starvation, and deportation. The sixth count in the indictment dealt with the general persecution of Jews on national, racial, religious, and political grounds. The seventh point dealt with the spoliation of Jewish property by inhuman measures, involving compulsion, robbery, terrorism, and violence. The eighth count of the indictment set forth that all these acts were, under our [Israeli] law, punishable war crimes.

There were also four charges that dealt with the systematic extermination of non-Jewish peoples — the Poles, Slovenes, Gypsies, and a special group of about 100 Czechoslovakian children. The last three charges concerned Eichmann's active membership in three Nazi organizations that had been declared criminal at the Nuremberg trials — the Gestapo (the Nazi secret police), the SS (Hitler's private police guard), and the SD (the intelligence division of the SS).

As the proceedings began, the world waited for Eichmann's words. Would he plead "guilty" and throw himself on the mercy of the court? Or would he sternly face his accusers and plead "not guilty"?

He did neither. His lawyer, Dr. Servatius, addressed the court and said that the defendant would not answer the charges, nor would he plead guilty or not guilty, until a ruling was made on whether or not the trial was legal. Dr. Servatius presented five main arguments against the basic legality of the trial.

1. Eichmann had been illegally kidnapped in order to be brought before the court.

2. The crimes with which he was charged had not been committed in Israel. It would be legal to try a person only in the country where the alleged crimes had been committed. Thus Eichmann should be tried in Germany, Russia, Poland, or Czechoslovakia, where his activities had purportedly been carried out.

3. Eichmann could not get a fair trial in Israel because witnesses for the defense would stay away, fearing for both their freedom and their physical safety in the country of Israel.
4. The judges would naturally be prejudiced. The crimes had been against the Jewish people; therefore, no Jewish judge could be impartial.
5. The crimes of which Eichmann was accused had not been crimes in Germany when he had committed them. They had been perfectly legal acts in that country at that particular time. Thus the crimes were *ex post facto*; that is, they had been declared crimes only *after* Eichmann had acted.

The prosecution answered each point as follows:

1. There were legal precedents in both the United States and England for bringing persons to trial, even though the means of apprehending them had not been legal. In an international trial of this nature, the defendant and his or her crimes — not the method of apprehension — were the important issue.
2. The other affected countries — Germany, Russia, Poland, etc. — had not requested the removal of Eichmann to their territory for trial. Since these nations did not wish to act on the matter, it became perfectly justified for Israel to take on the responsibility of holding the trial.
3. Since it was agreed that defense witnesses could testify by written deposition, they would not have to come to Israel to testify and were therefore free to give testimony in safety.

4. The judges were there solely to judge, from the evidence, whether Eichmann had or had not committed the crimes of which he was accused. They were not there to evaluate or pass judgment on the crimes themselves.

5. The question of the crimes being *ex post facto* had been dealt with at the Nuremberg trials. There it had been decided that if certain acts — such as the extermination of innocent human beings — are obviously immoral and illegal, then they are crimes even when the country wherein they are committed classifies them as legal. In effect, every person is responsible for his or her *own* actions in matters of basic human morality.

The arguments were well made on both sides. But they were stronger on the part of the prosecution, and there appeared to be clear legal justification for the trial. The judges ruled in favor of the prosecution, and the trial proceeded.

The problems the prosecution faced in presenting its case were immense. They are best described, however, in a simple one-sentence question asked by prosecutor Gideon Hausner: "How does one speak for six million dead?"

In his opening remarks to the court, Hausner did that to the best of his ability. He began by describing the enormity of the crimes themselves. Then he described Adolf Eichmann's position and duties in the Third Reich: he was the man directly in charge of carrying out the program against the Jews. Hausner then ended with a review of the charges and with a description of the evidence that he intended to present at the trial.

Adolf Eichmann sat in his glass booth, listening

Adolf Eichmann

intently to the proceedings of the court. He showed no
emotion whatsoever as his crimes were described. Occa-
sionally he would shake his head, but that was all. He
watched as witness after witness was brought before the
court. Each told of the horrors of the death camps.
People spoke of seeing husbands, wives, and children
murdered. Some described how the Jews were lined up in
front of open pits and machine-gunned down, and how
others were led into gas chambers and murdered there
by the thousands. There were stories of the terrible medical experiments conducted on human beings and of the
great ovens in which the dead bodies were cremated. The
witnesses recounted every chapter of the ghastly story.

Documentary evidence was submitted to show that Eichmann had participated in the "final solution" from the very beginning. He had been present at the Wannsee Conference outside Berlin, in 1942, where the plan had originally been put into operation. Documents also showed that he had participated in practically every aspect of the program's operation. His signature appeared on many orders to carry out the terrible deeds. The amount of documentary evidence that showed Eichmann's involvement in the crimes was gigantic.

The prosecution also presented witnesses who linked Eichmann directly with the carrying out of the "final solution." One witness even described how Eichmann had personally beaten a young Jewish boy to death.

Victims of Nazi brutality. These unburied bodies were found by American soldiers near the Buchenwald concentration camp in Germany.

Spectators listen solemnly to the accounts of witnesses during the Eichmann trial.

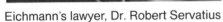
Eichmann's lawyer, Dr. Robert Servatius   Prosecutor Gideon Hausner

Dr. Robert Servatius then spoke for the defense. In his opening remarks, he presented the case for Adolf Eichmann.

The defense will show that the involvement of the accused in the persecution of the Jews was a necessity...a result that could not be avoided...the responsibility lies on the shoulders of the political leadership of the country....All the government apparatus was a partner, and all had a hand in this terrible harvest....The defense will prove that the accused is not responsible for the exterminations... that he did not give the order and was not the executor...that as far as he was concerned, there was no possibility for him to refuse orders....

The defense made no effort to deny that the crimes had been committed. Nor did the defense deny that Adolf Eichmann had been involved with them. The case for the defense was simply that Adolf Eichmann was only a minor official with no authority to create policy. He had simply carried out the orders of his superiors as he had been trained to do since childhood.

Then Adolf Eichmann took the stand in his own defense, although he actually spoke from inside the bullet-proof glass booth. He tried to explain his role in the Third Reich. He blamed the crimes he had committed on those above him in authority. He also said that many of the acts had been performed by people below him who, he said, received orders directly from his superiors. He maintained that, therefore, he had had no part in those actions. As to the written evidence, he said either that it was wrong or that it had been forged. In addition, he said that either the eyewitnesses were mistaken, or they simply wanted *some* German — any German — to suffer for the crimes that had been committed. He was their scapegoat. Then, Eichmann even implied that he had tried to help many Jews. In an attempt perhaps to win sympathy from the court, he once went so far as to say, "I declare that I regard the murder of the Jews as one of the greatest crimes in human history." Perhaps for the first and only time in the long trial, everyone in the courtroom agreed with Adolf Eichmann.

Eichmann was cross-examined both by the prosecutor, Gideon Hausner, and by the three judges on the bench. He held to his story, even though in many cases it was self-contradictory. Often he simply said that certain evidence was "wrong" or that he just "could not remember."

After the cross-examination, at which he made a rather

The three judges at Eichmann's trial. Judge Moshe Landau *(above)*, Dr. Yitzhak Raveh *(below, left)*, Dr. Benjamin Halevy *(below, right)*.

poor showing, the testimony of the defense witnesses was introduced. Their evidence, however, turned out to be mostly a defense of their own actions rather than a defense of Adolf Eichmann. Hence, their testimony had little effect on the court. The defense then rested its case.

The trial of Adolf Eichmann had lasted 14 weeks. After hearing all the evidence, the judges retired for 4 months to reach their decision. On December 11, 1961, exactly 8 months from the day the trial had begun, they announced their verdict.

No one was really surprised that Eichmann was found guilty. But everyone asked what kind of punishment could be meted out to a man guilty of the murders of six million humans? The answer, of course, was that no punishment on earth is equal such a horrendous crime. The most severe penalty under the law is death, and death was the sentence pronounced on Adolf Eichmann.

The judges' decision and the sentence were appealed, but the appeals were refused.

On May 31, 1962, Adolf Eichmann was hanged in Israel. His last words were "Long live Germany...Argentina ...Austria...I shall not forget them....I had to obey the rules of war and my flag." Like so many of the Jews he had caused to die, he was cremated the following day.

The trial is over now. Adolf Eichmann is dead. The controversy about the kidnapping of Eichmann, too, is for the most part forgotten. But the crimes that he committed will never be forgotten, nor should they be. For the vivid memory of such horrors may serve to warn people and governments against allowing such a thing ever to happen again.

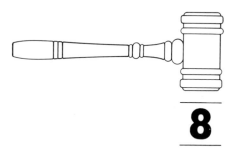

8

Anatoly Shcharansky

In July 1978, the Soviet authorities were leading Anatoly Shcharansky into the Moscow courtroom for his trial when his brother Leonid caught a glimpse of him. It was the first time Leonid had seen his brother since Anatoly's arrest 16 months earlier. Now Anatoly's captors marched him toward the grim courtroom with its barred windows. All but a few spectators, hand-picked by the government, were forbidden entry to the trial.

"You got fat!" Anatoly teased, as the guards hurried him past his brother. The remark was characteristic of Anatoly; still it was unexpected, coming from a man about to go on trial for his life on a charge of treason against his country. But then, Anatoly Shcharansky was not a man to be easily frightened by his circumstances. He had been openly challenging the Soviet regime for years. In a nation where being a good citizen meant being a quiet and obedient citizen, Anatoly Shcharansky was a very troublesome person to have around.

In April 1975, Anatoly Shcharansky *(third from left)* celebrated a birthday with some friends in Moscow. Three years later, two members of the group, Vladimir Slepak *(far right)* and his wife, Maria *(far left)*, were arrested for publicly displaying a banner that read, "Let us go to our son in Israel." Vladimir Slepak was exiled to Siberia for five years.

Anatoly Shcharansky was a 30-year-old Ukrainian-born Jew. He had been trained as a mathematician and computer expert, but he had been unemployed since 1973. That year, he had applied for permission to emigrate from the Soviet Union to Israel. He had been turned down on the grounds that his work involved knowledge of "state secrets." Since that time, Shcharansky had become a leader in the Soviet dissident movement, acting as a spokesman for other Jewish *refusniks* (Jews whose applications to emigrate had been refused). In addition, he had participated in unofficial groups that acted as "Helsinki monitors." These monitors were Soviet citizens who spoke out publicly against Soviet violations of the 1975 Helsinki Agreement. The agreement was a pledge made by the United States, Canada, Russia, and 31 nations of Europe, in Helsinki, Finland. In it these nations agreed to provide basic human rights — rights such as the freedom to emigrate, to practice one's religion, to speak freely, and even to criticize the government — to all their citizens. But many people charged that the Russians had gone back on their word and were ignoring the agreement.

Together with the trial of Anatoly Shcharansky, the Soviet Union was staging several other trials to take place at the same time. One hundred miles southwest of Moscow in Kaluga, Aleksandr Ginzburg went on trial. Ginzburg had already served two-year and five-year prison terms for dissident activities in the 1960s. He had been punished then for having published *samizdat* — unauthorized "underground" publications — concerning the trials of other dissident writers. This time when he was arrested he was a member of a Helsinki monitoring group. In addition, he was acting as an administrator of a fund set up by Nobel Prize winner and Soviet expatriate Aleksandr Solzhenitsyn. The money was being used by Ginzburg to help feed and clothe families of Soviet political prisoners. Ginzburg also helped these families to visit their relatives far away in Siberian prison camps. The Soviet government accused Ginzburg of "anti-Soviet agitation and propaganda," and charged him with spending the money on liquor and women.

A third dissident, Viktoras Petkus, went on trial at the same time in Vilnius, Lithuania. Petkus was a longtime Roman Catholic activist living under a government that frowned on religion. He had already served 16 years in various prison camps because of his religious activities. Petkus had become an organizer of a Lithuanian committee to monitor the Helsinki Agreement. He was charged with "anti-Soviet agitation."

Soviet dissident and Nobel Prize winner
Aleksandr Solzhenitsyn

To emphasize the seriousness of the fate that could await the dissidents, the Soviet government staged a fourth trial. Anatoly Filatov, who was not a known dissident and who may have actually been a spy, was tried for high treason. He was described by the Russians as an agent of an unnamed foreign power. The Soviet government accused Filatov of having in his possession miniature cameras, a miniature radio disguised as a cigarette lighter, and other devices that appeared to be spy equipment. Filatov was convicted and sentenced to death by firing squad.

The Soviet government apparently had a number of motives for staging trials of the dissidents at this time. For one thing, the government wanted to crush dissent within the Soviet Union. The Soviets believed that the best endorsement of the communist system was to present a united front to the free world. Thus the dissidents were a great embarrassment to the government. They were living testimony to the fact that there were Soviet citizens who were unhappy with the communist system and wanted to leave the country. If the Soviets permitted such outspoken criticism to go unchecked, the dissidents' attitudes could spread and threaten the stability of the government itself.

In the past, Russian policy toward dissidents had varied over the years in response to the shifting world political climate. At times the Soviet attitude had been somewhat relaxed, and dissidents had been allowed to leave the country. Yet these 1978 dissident trials indicated that the Russians were switching back to a hard-line attitude. In trying to make an example of Shcharansky, Ginzburg, and Petkus, the government was delivering a message to other dissidents that similar behavior would be punished severely. The Russians wanted all dissidents to know that there was no way the United States government, or anyone else, could help them.

Many observers felt that the Soviet government also had foreign policy reasons, not only for staging these trials but also for holding them at the particular time they chose. The trials took place at exactly the same time that delicate negotiations between the United States and the Soviet Union were under way. A series of these negotiations had been going on between the two governments since 1969. Referred to as "SALT" (Strategic Arms Limitation Talks), they were attempts to limit the production of nuclear weapons by the two superpowers. Throughout the Cold War years, the two nations had run an "arms race" in which each had built up greater and greater stores of expensive and destructive nuclear weapons. In 1969 the two had nearly equal striking capabilities, and they decided to try to slow down this costly "race." Several rounds of negotiations had gone on since then, with varying degrees of success. In 1978 the two superpowers planned to meet again in Geneva, Switzerland, for further talks.

Some people argued that the Soviet government officials wished to test United States attitudes toward these negotiations by conducting trials that they knew would outrage the American public. The Soviets reasoned that American reaction to the trials would give them a hint about how the United States might behave during the SALT talks. The Russians guessed further that despite the public's outrage about the trials, the American government would not go so far as to cancel or postpone the talks in protest. Their guess was correct. The Soviets now saw how eager the United States was to hold the SALT talks. If the Americans were that eager, they might also be ready to make important concessions to the Russians during the talks. Knowing this ahead of time gave the Soviets a great bargaining advantage in Geneva.

Observers saw another important foreign policy advantage that Russia hoped to gain over the United States by conducting these trials. The trials of Jewish dissidents might give the Russians an edge in dealing with oil-rich Arab nations. Both Shcharansky and Ginzburg were from Jewish backgrounds. Shcharansky was a Jew, and Ginzburg, though a member of the Russian Orthodox faith, had had a Jewish mother. By putting these men on trial, perhaps the Russians sought to win favor with Arab states that were unfriendly to Israel. In addition, the Russians may have reasoned that the United States government would be sympathetic to Shcharansky and Ginzburg, and that such an attitude would anger the Arabs.

Many people also saw the trials as an attempt to embarrass President Carter and weaken him politically in the United States. One of the major themes of President

Carter's administration had been his emphasis on human rights abroad. In the dissident trials, the defendants were denied the right to select a lawyer, to use cross-examination, to call witnesses on their own behalf, to be tried in an open courtroom, or to receive a jury verdict. These are all elements regarded as essential to a fair trial in the United States. In addition, the very acts for which the defendants were being tried were their energetic public statements in defense of the human rights promised them under the Helsinki Agreement — an agreement signed by their own government. The Soviet Union was, in effect, saying to the president of the United States, "Now you have made a big fuss about the human rights policies of other governments. If you don't like *ours*, just what are you going to do about it?"

Though many urged him to call off the SALT talks as a protest against the trials, President Carter decided against such a drastic step. Instead, the president responded to the trials by cancelling sales of computers and oil-drilling equipment to the Russians as a measure of American disapproval.

Meanwhile, the trial of Anatoly Shcharansky began. Since the courtroom was closed to the public, the details of this proceeding will probably always be a mystery. We know that Shcharansky was charged with "anti-Soviet agitation" because of his activities in the dissident movement. He was also charged with treason and espionage. The Soviets said that he had supplied "state secrets… to an agent of a foreign intelligence service who worked under cover of a journalist in Moscow." Shcharansky had, in fact, supplied lists of names and addresses of refusniks to Robert Toth, a reporter for the *Los Angeles Times*. But the list that Shcharansky had furnished Toth

107

was not a "state secret" under Soviet law. All the refusniks had been officially notified by the government that they had been refused their emigration rights. All were free under Russian law to tell that fact to the press. If any state secrets had been revealed, the Soviet authorities had done it themselves when they had notified the refusniks that the factories they worked in were involved in state secrets. But then, of course, the real point of the trial was not to punish Anatoly Shcharansky for revealing state secrets, but to punish him for being a thorn in the side of the Soviet government.

In the courtroom where Shcharansky was being tried, no Western journalists were allowed. Twice daily a Soviet spokesman read reporters a short official account of the proceedings inside. The spokesman refused to answer any questions. Even Shcharansky's mother was barred from attending the trial or from catching a glimpse of her son as he was carted back and forth between the courtroom and the prison. Shcharansky's brother Leonid, however, was permitted to attend several sessions of the trial.

Since a defense lawyer works only with the consent and under the control of the government in the Soviet Union, Shcharansky preferred to dismiss the lawyer appointed to him and to defend himself. But he was not permitted to call any witnesses of his own, or to cross-examine those called against him. His brother Leonid reported that Anatoly had insisted in court that the charges were "absurd" and had said, "I do not acknowledge any guilt." And apparently, the prosecution was unable to produce evidence of any classified information that Shcharansky had furnished to Toth or to anyone else. Yet it seemed obvious what the verdict would be, even though the case against Shcharansky was so weak.

Anatoly Shcharansky's wife, Avital, left the Soviet Union for Israel in July 1974, expecting that her husband would join her there shortly. Since Anatoly's arrest, Avital has traveled throughout the West urging political and business leaders to help free her husband.

The trial took four days. The verdict was announced by the judge, who was a member of the Communist party, as are all judges in the Soviet Union. He had been assisted by two nonprofessional "people's assessors," also Party members. The verdict was, of course, guilty of treason, espionage, and "anti-Soviet agitation." The sentence was 13 years in prison and labor camps — the most serious sentence that can be handed down under Soviet law short of the death penalty.

The next day in Kaluga, Aleksandr Ginzburg was sentenced to 8 years at hard labor. Like Shcharansky, Ginzburg had remained defiant throughout his trial. When asked his nationality he had replied, "*Zeka*" ("prisoner"). In Vilnius, Petkus also got a stiff sentence — 10 years in prison and 5 years of Siberian exile. During his trial, Petkus lay down in the witness box with his eyes closed and refused to participate in the proceedings.

In a single week's time, the Soviet government had managed to rid itself of 3 of its most prominent trouble-makers. Of the 38 members of the Helsinki monitoring groups who are now identified, 24 have emigrated or are in prison or in exile. More trials are expected. The trials clearly demonstrate the hard-line attitude that the government is now taking toward individual expression of dissent and dissatisfaction in the Soviet Union. As one Soviet official so aptly explained, "Soviet law is the means by which the will of the dominant class is expressed.

Aleksandr Ginzburg, shown here with his wife and two sons, came to the United States on April 27, 1979. Ginzburg and four other dissidents were permitted to leave the Soviet Union in exchange for the release of two Soviet spies imprisoned in the United States.

Index

Act of Supremacy, 27
Andrassy Street prison, 75, 76, 77, 81

Ben-Gurion, David, 83
Biddle, Francis, 65
Boleyn, Anne, 26, 27
bordereau in Dreyfus case, 47, 48, 50
Bormann, Martin, 61, 63, 71
brainwashing, 76
Burgundy, duke of, 8, 12, 13, 20

Carter, Jimmy, 106-107
Catherine of Aragon, 25-26, 27
Cauchon, Pierre, 14, 19
Charles VII (king of France), 8-10, 12, 15, 16, 20
Chinon, castle of, 9
Cold War, 72-73, 77, 80
common law, English, 30
Communism: in eastern Europe, 72, 73; in Hungary, 75, 79; in the Soviet Union, 104-105
concentration camps, 56, 57, 59, 84, 87, 94
Copernicus, Nicolaus, 36, 37, 39, 41
court-martial, 45
courts, political use of, 5-7
Cranmer, Thomas, 27

Demange, Charles, 48
Devil's Island, 49, 51
Dialogue on the Two Principal Systems of the World, 37-38
dissidents, Soviet policy toward, 104-106
Dönitz, Karl, 62, 71
Donnedieu de Vabre, Henri, 65

Erasmus, 24
Esterhazy, Ferdinand, 47, 50, 51, 52
ex post facto crimes, 69, 92, 93

Filatov, Anatoly, 104
Fisher, John, 28, 29, 30
France, Anatole, 51
Frank, Hans, 63
freedom fighters, Hungarian, 79-80
Frick, Wilhelm, 63
Fritsche, Hans, 63, 71
Funk, Walther, 63, 71

Gestapo, 61, 91
Gide, André, 51
Ginzburg, Aleksandr, 103, 105, 109, 110
Goebbels, Joseph, 59
Göring, Hermann, 60-61, 71, 87

Halevy, Benjamin, 89
Hapsburg, Otto, 75
Hausner, Gideon, 89-90, 93, 98
Helsinki Agreement, 102-103
Henry, Hubert, 47, 50, 52
Henry VIII (king of England), 23, 25-27, 28, 31
Henry VI (king of England), 13, 14
heresy, crime of, 14, 39-41
Hess, Rudolph, 62, 71
Himmler, Heinrich, 59
Hitler, Adolph, 55, 56, 57, 59
Holbein the younger, Hans, 24
Hundred Years' War, 8, 12, 20

inquisitors of Roman Catholic church, 14, 15, 39-40
international law, 69
iron curtain, 73

Jackson, Robert H., 65, 66
Jews, persecution of, during World War II, 55, 56, 57, 58, 66, 82, 84, 90-91, 94
Jodl, Alfred, 62
John of Luxembourg, 12
jurisdiction of courts, 6

Kaltenbrunner, Ernst, 62
Keitel, Wilhelm, 62
Klement, Ricardo, 82
Krupp, Gustav, 63

Landau, Moshe, 89
Lawrence, Geoffrey, 65
Le Maistre, Jean, 15
Ley, Robert, 63
Lippershey, Hans, 35
London Agreement, 58-59, 64
Luftwaffe, 61
Luther, Martin, 26

Menthon, François de, 65
Mercier, Auguste, 49, 52

Nazi party, 55, 56
Neurath, Constantin von, 63, 71
Nikitichenko, I. T., 65
Nuremberg Decrees, 55

Papen, Franz von, 63, 71
Paul V (pope), 36, 41
Petkus, Viktoras, 103, 105,
    109-110
Picquart, Georges, 50
Pius XII (pope), 74
planets, motions of, 35-36
Proust, Marcel, 51

Orléans, battle of, 10

Raeder, Erich, 62, 71
Raveh, Yitzhak, 89
refusniks, 102, 107-108
Ribbentrop, Joachim von, 61-62

Roman Catholic church: and
    Galileo, 5, 33, 36-44; and
    Henry VIII, 25-27; inquisitors
    of, 14, 15, 39-40; and Joan
    of Arc, 14, 15, 19, 21; and
    Thomas More, 24, 27, 31
Rosenberg, Alfred, 62
Rudenko, R. A., 65

samizdat, 103
Sauckel, Fritz, 62
Schacht, Hjalmar, 63, 71
Schirach, Baldur von, 62, 71
Servatius, Robert, 89, 91, 97
Seyss-Inquart, Artur, 63
Shawcross, Sir Hartley, 65
Shcharansky, Avital, 109
Shcharansky, Leonid, 101, 108
"show trial," 6
Sidereal Message, 36
Slepak, Vladimir, 102
Solzhenitsyn, Aleksandr, 103
Speer, Albert, 62, 71
SS (Hitler's private guard), 59, 91
Strategic Arms Limitation Talks
    (SALT), 105, 106, 107
Streicher, Julius, 62

telescope, Galileo's use of, 35, 36
torture used to obtain confessions,
    14, 18, 76

Urban VIII (pope), 37-38
Utopia, 24

war crimes, definition of, 59, 60
World War II, 55, 56-57, 72

Zola, Émile, 51-52